HOW TO GET
GOOD CARE
SERVICES

If you want to know how...

The Carer's Handbook

The Parent's Guide to Childcare

Choosing a Care Home

Fundraising for a Community Project

How To Pay Less for More

howtobooks

Send for a free copy of the latest catalogue to:

How To Books
Spring Hill House, Spring Hill Road, Begbroke
Oxford OX5 1RX. United Kingdom.
email: info@howtobooks.co.uk
www.howtobooks.co.uk

HOW TO GET
GOOD CARE
SERVICES

For yourself or your relatives

CLARE KIRKMAN

howtobooks

Published by How To Books Ltd,
Spring Hill House, Spring Hill Road,
Begbroke, Oxford OX5 1RX, United Kingdom.
Tel: (01865) 375794. Fax: (01865) 379162.
email: info@howtobooks.co.uk
www.howtobooks.co.uk

How To Books greatly reduce the carbon footprint of their books by sourcing their
typesetting and printing in the UK.

British Library Cataloguing in Publication Data
A catalogue record for this book is available from the British Library

ISBN 978 1 84528 243 1

Cover design by Baseline Arts Ltd, Oxford
Produced for How To Books by Deer Park Productions, Tavistock, Devon
Typeset by PDQ Typesetting, Newcastle-under-Lyme, Staffs.
Printed and bound by Bell & Bain Ltd, Glasgow

NOTE: The material contained in this book is set out in good faith for general guidance
and no liability can be accepted for loss or expense incurred as a result of relying in
particular circumstances on statements made in the book. Laws and regulations are
complex and liable to change, and readers should check the current position with the
relevant authorities before making personal arrangements.

Contents

Part 2 Know the Minimum Standards

Introduction

Arranging health or social care services can be challenging. The failure or success of choices made will affect your life, *or* if you are arranging care on behalf of someone else, their life. Such effects could be significant now or in the future.

The aim of this book is to:

- minimise the challenges
- simplify the planning process
- show you how to obtain relevant information – informing choices
- heighten consumer awareness
- help you to recognise a quality care service
- maximise your potential to find the right service from the outset.

The average person knows very little about identifying a quality or value-for-money service, yet billions of pounds are spent on health and social care services annually.

> **IT'S A FACT!**
> Social care is one of the fastest growing service sectors in the country and is set to continue to grow.

CONSUMER AWARENESS IS RARE

Consumer awareness informs us of our rights and choices. We are free to shop around for similar goods or services of varying prices and quality. With freedom to choose where to spend our money, mainstream organisations remain competitive both in terms of standard of product/service and value or risk losing custom. If, having made a purchase, our goods or service are substandard, we also have some legal protection. Consumers can be reasonably demanding and many businesses are responsive to feedback and will further develop their organisations to meet consumer expectations.

There are several facts that make being a consumer of health and social care services more complex than when consuming any other goods or services.

- There is a *need* for a care service and this in itself can limit choice. If there simply isn't an alternative service with which one can make comparisons when help is required, then the *available* service is usually purchased. For example, there may be only one care home within a town or village.

- On occasion a service may have to be arranged at speed and consumers simply choose any service that is available to help. However, some people are apprehensive to start the planning process all over again even if once using a service bought in haste; they realise that they are not completely happy.

- Many people in receipt of care are so grateful to have it that they make 'excuses' for poor service, thus rarely challenging it or giving permission for anyone else to do so on their behalf.

- There have been few representative voices on the issue of consumer awareness for those buying health and social care services.

But times are changing and in response to an increased need for services, the sector is expanding, and small private and large corporate organisations are opening with regularity. With industry growth is coming greater competition which in turn is influencing and pushing up standards of service, forcing a better value-for-money pricing policy and an increased availability of care. These facts combined should mean a better range of choice for consumers. Following the introduction of tighter regulation of care services, measurable quality control methods are now also in place adding further power to those buying into them.

The regulation of services includes an obligation for organisations to adhere to the National Minimum Care Standards (NMCS), which are quite simply what they say – a set of standards below which providers of services must not allow their provision of care to fall.

Care organisations are currently inspected by the Commission for Social Care Inspection (CSCI), although there are plans for the CSCI to merge with the Healthcare Commission and Mental Health Act Commission, creating a new inspection body and will do so sometime after April 2009. I explain in more detail about the current and future health and social care inspection process in Chapter 11. But in brief, the introduction of regulation means that not only do you have a right to expect a certain standard of care and service, but you have recourse if the obligations of an organisation are not met. I provide an overview of the National Minimum Care Standards used by the CSCI during inspection and this information will act as a useful tool not only during our planning stages but will enable you to continually monitor and evaluate the quality of service eventually bought.

WHERE DO YOU START?

Initially, you must decide on the type of care preferred and then choose an organisation to provide it. But as there are numerous types of care service the options can become confusing. Choices at first appear to be limited to those of either a residential/nursing home or care provided within a person's own home. Yet each service is unique and even if looking for a service within the same category, you will quickly learn that each organisation is different. Some domiciliary care providers, for example, will offer a complete 'care service' while others act as 'agents'.

Would you know the difference between the two and how those differences might affect you?

- Diversity of choice is important but with choice can come information overload, especially as buying a care service is not something you will do every day.

- It is not like buying a product that can be touched and examined for quality. Advice given by a care organisation about whether theirs is the best service for the potential consumer may not always be objective or relevant.

- Advice given by professionals (such as social workers) may be given based on professional guidance, the reality of which will include budgetary constraints, as opposed to advice that is purely in the best interests of the person requiring care. In support of this statement visit http://www.csci.org.uk – view ALL NEWS – then go through the pages which list news in date order, starting with the most recent. Find an article dated 18 October 2006 and read the report called 'Time to care'.

As a modern consumer of care services, you must take control of the planning process. I therefore explain where you can *find* care services and how to *recognise* quality care versus poor. I cover many practical points that need to be considered in addition to whether a service can provide the physical help required. For example:

- Does an organisation have suitably qualified staff to care for the physical needs of the person requiring care?

- Will emotional needs, likes, dislikes and preferences be respected?

- Does the organisation take responsibility if care workers break an object of value belonging to the person receiving the care?

- How much notice would an organisation require to terminate a service agreement?

- Do standard terms and conditions apply to all care organisations within the UK?

- Under what circumstances does a care organisation waiver their cancellation fee?

Apart from the obvious physical benefits of choosing a care service in which you have confidence, research conducted by the CSCI showed those in receipt of good care services felt that in the event of problems the provider would 'sort things out' for them. The same research also found that people unhappy with their standard of care or those less able to articulate their views did not share that confidence. This research is a strong indication that the providers of good care will always have a clear complaints procedure, contrasting sharply with providers of *substandard services,* as consumers of such services lack confidence or have no idea how to complain effectively. To maximise your chances of entering into an agreement with a reliable organisation, I will help you to satisfy yourself that potential providers handle complaints effectively.

We will look at which professionals can support choices and in some cases, highlight the responsibilities they have towards individuals planning and/or requiring care.

Together let us show providers of care that consumers want to spend their money wisely, that they know their rights and that they are not afraid to demand quality care.

Providers of care, BEWARE – care consumers are fully AWARE.

Clare Kirkman

Note

If you live in Scotland, Wales or Northern Ireland these countries have their own regulatory bodies, but the standards are national and the planning principles remain the same.

Part 1

Practical Steps to Finding Good Services

Finding Services

Physical health will influence the type of care a person requires, but it should not be the only factor when considering the most appropriate service. For example, some medical professionals may give an opinion that 'medically' a move into a nursing home is the right care solution for an older person, but that opinion should not automatically remove a person's right to choice.

REMEMBER
A *qualification* does not necessarily *qualify* a professional to know which type of care is right for the person requiring it.

There are ways that an individual can be cared for within their own home even with high-level medical needs if that is where they want to be.

So when at the planning stages of arranging a care service, think laterally about *circumstances as a whole* rather than focusing solely on *healthcare needs.*

POINTS TO CONSIDER WHEN PLANNING A CARE SERVICE

The following questions are in no order of importance nor by any means exhaustive. They are merely a starting point to provoke thought.

- **Personal preference**. Would staying at home be practical? If so, what level of care would be required?

- **Age of person.** Does the choice of care organisation have workers who are trained to care for a specific age group?

- **Children.** Does the person requiring care have young children or is a child themselves? Will this further limit care choices?

- **Personality**. If living in a care or group home is preferred, would a family-run business or one with the ambience of a quality hotel be the ideal place?

- **Background**. Is the individual insular and, if so, would one-on-one care be a better choice and how could that be achieved?

- **Social status**. A high-flying lifestyle of exquisite restaurants or a down-to-earth working-class individual? How might social standing influence care choices?

- **Religious and cultural beliefs**. There may be important issues such as how a person dresses, diet, timetable, social calendar, etc. that need to be considered. How would the chosen care organisation continue to meet these needs?

- **Sexual orientation**. Would a transgender/gay or lesbian person feel that their needs are fully understood?

- **Physical limitations**. If an individual has physical limitations, might such limitations appear to restrict choice, making a care home seem the only valid option? Might equipment in the home make staying tenable?

- **Long-term prognosis**. Is there a terminal condition and, if so, how will quality of life be affected by care choices?

- **Lifestyle**. Smoker/drinker/pet owner? Will care choices compromise lifestyle?

- **Cost of service/funding available**. Who will pay for the care and how will this influence choices?

- **Support available from family and friends**. What support can family and friends offer, if any, to facilitate choices?

CHOOSING THE APPROPRIATE TYPE OF CARE

You may have a clear idea of the type of care preferred or you may still be unsure. At this very early stage of planning uncertainty is natural and a lot may depend on whether you are arranging care for yourself, on behalf of a family member or friend or in a professional capacity. Choices will also be strongly influenced by whether care is for an elderly person, a young adult or a child, and will be dependent on the dynamics of their relationships and responsibility towards others. For example, if care is sought for an adult with multiple sclerosis and the individual is married with children, is a long-term care home really a viable option?

Whatever your situation, I discourage you from closing your mind to the possibility of *any type* of care until all options have been given careful consideration.

I cover the most common services available and split them into two main categories – *care homes* and *domiciliary care* – with sub-categories within each.

Care homes

Care homes (the standards for this category include homes for young adults and those with learning disabilities) are:

- residential homes
- nursing homes.

Domiciliary care

Domiciliary care (this category of service does include registration for those providing services to children and their families) are:

- daily care
- live-in care
- employment agencies.

Respite and rehabilitation are addressed in Chapters 6 and 7 on care home and domiciliary care choices as they can be facilitated in either.

Also, Chapter 8 includes extensive information on **privately employing a care worker** for readers wishing to recruit their own workers.

Note

If you are recruiting private care as part of a 'brokerage scheme' then visit the CSCI's website http://www.csci.org.uk, follow the link for 'care provider' and read the latest guidance to clarify whether you will need to register with the Commission.

Now let us look at how to find care services.

SOCIAL SERVICES

In an ideal world, Social Services would be the first point of contact because they can assist with arranging health and social care even if they are not paying for it.

Unfortunately, many social workers have to work with increasing amounts of red tape and lack of resources and whether care is required for children, older people or adults with disabilities will influence the amount of money available to spend. The geographical area can also have an influence on available funding because some local authorities have more cash available than others.

I do not wish to add to the already overburdened resources of Social Services by insisting that everyone requiring care rushes to their local authority for an assessment but you should feel free to do so. However, there are situations when I would *strongly recommend* that even if care is likely to be self-funded, Social Services should *always be involved.* These are:

■ When someone is providing unpaid care to loved ones/ relatives or neighbours and they require a break. Social services may be able to fund/assist with respite help.

■ If a person requiring care does not have immediate family or friends to monitor their well-being.

■ When a professional without healthcare experience has arranged care for a third party, e.g. a solicitor who organises care for an elderly client through their power of attorney and, once care is organised, they withdraw their involvement.

IT'S A FACT

In June 2007 the 13th annual Carers Week, a week dedicated to raising awareness of what carers do and celebrating the contribution they make in our
communities, was held. The publicity generated during Carers Week enables
tens of thousands more carers to be contacted and told about the support and
services available to them. A dedicated website (www.newdealforcarers.org) will
allow carers and professionals to feed in their views on how to improve carers'
lives. This is a welcome development as too many carers are living in poverty,
giving up work, risking their health and finding themselves unable to prepare for
the future. Yet their contribution was, at the time of the 13th annual carers
week, worth £57bn.

Regardless of whether involved in planning, Social Services will
have a list of companies registered to provide care services and
should be able to recommend organisations within your area. Be
specific and ask social services for their experience of local care
providers, not just for telephone numbers. This could save you a
lot of time calling substandard organisations.

Funding of care services

If an assessment by social services is undertaken, it may be
decided that care services will be funded by the local authority. If
so then a review of that care should be carried out at least every 12
months or more regularly if there are issues or as problems arise.
In between reviews, social services representatives will take up
matters with the care providers on behalf of consumers should
they need to. They can also coordinate additional services such as
occupational therapists.

It is important to understand that *if* Social Services agree to fund
care, they will have some control over which services are used.

Direct payment scheme

There is also a *direct payment* scheme whereby the local authority passes directly to individuals funds which may be spent on any chosen care service, subject to some reasonable conditions. However, when older people require care, eligibility for direct payments becomes less common (but not unheard of) than when funding care for those aged 65 and under.

> **REMEMBER**
> Be a smart consumer and claim benefits to which you are entitled.

If in doubt as to whether you are eligible for funding you should call Social Services or an independent financial adviser with experience of care funding.

There are many non-means tested benefits that can be claimed even by those who have the resources to self-fund care.

COMMISSION FOR SOCIAL CARE INSPECTION

A brief overview of the Commission for Social Care Inspection (CSCI) can be found in the Introduction and Chapter 11.

As the organisation responsible for inspection and regulation of all care services throughout England, they hold a database of organisations registered to carry out the provision of care and all care services must be registered to legally operate.

> **Note**
> Scotland, Wales and Northern Ireland have their own inspection
> and regulatory bodies.

You should be looking to buy into organisations that generally
meet all of the National Minimum Care Standards but no service
will be perfect and some standards are more important than
others. You will know your own priorities and will naturally make
purchasing decisions based on these.

Searching the CSCI database

The CSCI database can be searched for:

■ Care homes with or without nursing and further broken down
   into categories of:
   – learning disability
   – old age only
   – sensory impairment
   – dementia (EMI)
   – mental health
   – physical disability
   – drug dependency
   – alcohol dependency.
■ Home care (domiciliary agencies).
■ Nurses agencies (private nursing for hospital or home care).
■ Adult placement schemes.

It can also be searched by:

■ postcode
■ region

■ name of care provider.

You can also conduct an independent search of the database online by going to:

■ www.csci.org.uk

or e-mailing:

■ enquiries@csci.gsi.gov.uk

or calling:

■ 0845 015 0120
■ 0191 233 3323

or textphone:

■ 0845 015 2255
■ 0191 233 3588

and a CSCI representative will undertake a search on your behalf. Alternatively, you may choose to make use of the database when you have identified service providers via another means.

Information held by the CSCI

If you choose to call the helpline, they should be able to give you information on services within your area. If you choose to research services online, you will see the site holds a considerable amount of information such as the following.

Past inspection reports

Although reading reports might be a tedious task for some, it would not be a wasted exercise. A copy of an inspection report will highlight issues of real relevance and the CSCI have made reports reader-friendly. You can view reports online by following the simple steps given on the site. You can search by company, or by finding a list of companies in your geographical area and then going through each company and their reports individually. You can print reports free of charge.

Alternatively you can obtain reports by:

■ Contacting a care company direct and asking if they can send you a copy of their latest report (which aside from the website may be the quickest option). Even if there is not a recent report showing on the website, the care provider will have received a copy very soon after inspection and unless they are disputing an inspector's findings, they should make a copy available to you.

■ If time permits, you can obtain free copies of reports from your local CSCI area office via the post.

When reading reports, you will see that CSCI use a star rating system indicating whether providers of care are meeting the required standards. The rating of a care organisation determines the frequency with which an organisation will be inspected. To a degree, the process of inspection is in some ways self-monitoring. I cover the inspection process in greater detail in Chapter 11.

Other information held by the CSCI

■ **Ownership of the company**. This section will tell you whether the care provider is privately owned or part of a larger organisation.

- **Registered manager's name**. This is an important point if you want to get straight to the top or know who has daily overall responsibility.

- **Contact details**. You can save time making contact with the relevant department if you have the correct contact details.

- **Category of care provided**. There is no point in pursuing a service that cannot provide for a person's needs. This is especially important if you are arranging services on behalf of children who are to be cared for at home or where a consumer of a service has children. All home care organisations with workers who have access to children must be registered to care for this user group and their workers must be trained in *child protection procedures*.

Even though CSCI information can assist with decision-making, there may be services that at the time of inspection had no visible flaws, but questions must still be asked because an inspection report is only a *snapshot* in time.

Inspection reports are made available to service providers *before* being made publicly available and they are given an opportunity to dispute facts. Therefore considerable weight must be given to this method of shortlisting services.

LOCAL GPs

Local GPs might have an association with care providers in their area and may have met some of the care workers or had dealings with managers of the service regarding their patients' health. GPs may therefore hold a valuable view on the quality of local care services.

SOLICITORS

Solicitors can have some form of power of attorney for people who require care but are without family or close friends. Some solicitors may have been involved in the planning of care and may have access to the names of service provisions they have used in the past or are actively using.

HOSPITAL DISCHARGE TEAMS

If a hospital has indicated that a care service is required in order that an individual be discharged from hospital, then the discharge team should undertake an 'assessment of need'. If they do not offer this, request one.

The assessment will be conducted by an employee of the hospital qualified in the process and is usually followed up with an occupational therapist's assessment. Both assessments will help to determine what level of care is required.

The point of assessment is a good time to discuss preferences in respect of either a move into a residential/nursing facility or receiving care at home. The hospital may have worked with service providers during the discharge of previous patients and may have relevant information on local care companies.

PERSONAL RECOMMENDATION

Personal recommendations are a valuable means of accessing services.

DON'T THEY SAY?
Advertising is what they pay for
but
good publicity is what they pray for.

THE LADY MAGAZINE

The Lady is a weekly magazine available every Tuesday at most good newsagents or you can visit them at http://www.lady.co.uk.

The magazine, established in 1885, has an excellent vetting system in respect of care organisation advertisements. Such vetting will include that all advertisers must provide details of their registration and CSCI and therefore *The Lady* would be unlikely to carry advertisements for a non-registered company.

The number of care service advertisements can run into double figures, so you won't be short of choice.

Be aware though that there is not the same thorough vetting for *The Lady*'s private lineage advertisements, since the vetting of individuals would be an impossible task for the publication's staff to undertake.

If you are considering the route of privately employing a care worker then see Chapter 8 for my advice on safe recruitment practices. Responding to an individual advertising their services as a care worker in *any* publication is not something I would recommend.

TNT

This is a free publication distributed throughout London. Although this magazine provides the details of many care companies, they are usually advertising for workers, not aiming their advertisement at consumers. However, a copy of this magazine will provide you with insight as to how care companies attract their care workers. For example, do they use promises of riches or do they offer quality support and training. You will also find the organisations' contact details on the advertisement.

YELLOW PAGES

The traditional *Yellow Pages* will provide details of services in your area, but no more than that.

If you have access to the Internet, you can use another section of *Yellow Pages* simply called Yell. You will find this at http://www.yell.com. This is a useful resource allowing searches by region and type of care business. It provides links to the websites of cited companies (if they have a website) as well as general contact information.

2

What *Do* the Brochures Say?

Now you know how to find services, what information can you expect to receive from those organisations in which you have an interest?

THE STANDARD OF INFORMATION SUPPLIED

Well, there has to date been an unspoken arrogance among a small number of care providers in that they have taken advantage of the fact that, in some English counties, there is more demand than supply of care services. Such organisations have provided little or substandard information at the early stages of an enquiry because they have known that without any effort in this area, consumers have still bought into the service.

Thankfully, with the introduction of the National Minimum Care Standards (NMCS), has come a requirement for care providers to supply a minimum level of information to all potential consumers. Organisation should now provide details in relation to what their service can offer, its terms and conditions, insurance information and the groups of people catered for, for example those with dementia. Yet even with such requirements placed on them, the quality of information offered by some organisations is still varied. One can only hope that eventually all providers of services will supply thorough information at the enquiry stages.

RESPONSE RATES

Whether information is of sound quality may not be your only hurdle. Research undertaken for this chapter showed that getting a brochure in the first instance was the greatest challenge. Having requested 320 brochures from nursing and residential homes combined and 185 from domiciliary care organisations throughout England, the numbers received were disappointing.

From *care homes* only 110 (approximately one in three) brochures were received of which:

- four carried insufficient postage and had to be collected from the post office

- only a handful included fees

- many sent confusing guidance outlining how they assess their level of charges.

From *domiciliary organisations* 30 brochures were received (fewer than one in six) of which:

- one had inadequate postage

- a further 54 responses were received by e-mail (the initial enquiry was via this means, but a residential address was provided and a request specifically made that a brochure be sent by post)

- three *e-mailed* responses refused to provide information unless the name and address of the potential consumer was provided

- two organisations suggested looking at their website and contacting them again should the enquiry be taken any further

- twenty-two of the responses included a statement of purpose (the contents of which is explained further under 'Information' within both sets of standards) and an e-brochure

- eleven replies included just prices with no additional information

- only 14 responses were specific to the request (although e-mailed instead of posted) and two companies sent only a web link.

WHAT CAN CARE PROVIDERS GAIN FROM THIS?

This research has made me question exactly what some care providers can possibly gain from failing to give the most basic information in the initial stages of an enquiry. More importantly, it makes me wonder whether they give consideration to the effort that goes into researching care services. Do they realise how distressing it can be? If so, then surely they would want to make life easier for their potential new customers! The research also showed that some organisations are not adhering to the most basic of 'minimum care standards'. But such a blatant lack of consideration for all the above points merely adds to the argument that some care organisations will not automatically treat consumers with the respect they deserve and my solution is – do not spend money with these providers.

It appeared on closer inspection that responses from *domiciliary care* providers showed that they either have more access to or made better use of e-mails, as there were no responses received in this way from *care homes*.

HOW DO I RATE THE INFORMATION SUPPLIED?

In terms of presentation, some of the brochures received were glossy while others were not. I recognise that many organisations might feel their money better spent on consumers already in receipt of care than on extravagant literature. For this reason I was careful not to judge brochures solely on presentation, but more on content, clarity and quality of information.

The poorest brochure received does deserve to be judged on presentation though, as it was merely a few pieces of paper stapled together. It contained substandard information, grammatical errors and childlike condescending pictures. I would seriously question whether this care provider is aware of the negative impact that such a poor first impression gives. If this company cannot make the effort to present itself properly in the initial stages, what would its service be like? I also question whether on inspection of this service, the CSCI representative perused the literature?

Reading information received should be the first step to determining whether you take your enquiry further. Below is a selection of extracts from the brochures I have seen and my views about what they are *really* saying. I include these in a bid to encourage you to read purposefully and thoroughly the literature that you receive.

CARE HOMES

'Bathing is as much a way of relaxing as it is a matter of cleanliness – we ensure that bathing is the pleasure it should be.'

A fear many people have of care home living is that they will lose their right to individuality, choice and privacy. The quote indicates that this home recognises such fears and wishes to convey that their environment is one that will respect the consumer's right to enjoy their stay.

'All residents will be treated with dignity. They will be treated as adults and individuals. Their wishes as to how they choose to be addressed will be respected.'

While I appreciate that providers of care want consumers to know that they follow good practice, I think it is a shame that anyone in the twenty-first century could feel the need to have to say that they will treat people with dignity, as an adult and individual. Dignified and appropriate individual treatment of anyone, whatever age or physical ability, is a fundamental human right and should not need to be a selling point in a brochure.

'You may eat whenever you wish.'

Fantastic – this one is a bit like the bath quote in that it is showing you the flexibility of the service. Some homes will provide a timetable for meals with their brochure so do make sure that you read any provided as it will tell you a lot about the home. The most ridiculous timetable I saw was a home offering breakfast flexibly between 7 a.m. and 11 a.m. *but* lunch then served at a non-flexible 12 noon.

'Hot and cold drinks, sandwiches and biscuits are available DAY AND NIGHT.'

And the same home states that:

'Support, help and advice is offered in case of bereavement.'

This home sounds genuinely kind and caring and such small gestures make the difference between a *care home* and a *home that cares.*

'Depending on suitability, we value and welcome pets.'

Sometimes the thought of leaving a pet behind is enough to stop a person moving into a care home, so to know that some homes will accept pets can be helpful.

'All clothes should be washable as we don't have dry cleaning facilities. Because clothes are laundered more frequently and at higher temperatures – to avoid cross infection – it is inevitable that clothing will have to be replaced on a more regular basis than normal. Delicate fabrics can be laundered or dry cleaned at an extra charge.'

This brochure goes on to provide a list of appropriate clothing suggesting that residents bring eight of everything. I feel such statements to be patronising and unnecessary. There is nothing *inevitable* about washing at high temperatures that guarantees that clothes would need to be replaced more regularly. I'm also slightly confused by this information. At the beginning of the quote they say that they don't have dry cleaning facilities, yet go on to say you can have items dry cleaned at an extra charge. So maybe they don't have facilities on site, but they have access to them.

One London-based nursing home refers to their 'exquisite' lounge, which in the photograph shows an expanse of garish pub carpet and a pile of zimmer frames in the corner. Oh how tastes differ!

> *'Fees are reviewed bi-annually on 1st April and 1st October.'*

I would want to know if review has always resulted in a fee increase.

> *'The management reserve the right to move residents between rooms, for the benefit of the resident or to facilitate the efficient running of the home. Any damage or breakages by the resident will be expected to be replaced.'*

And the same home states:

> *'No refund will be given in respect of fees paid in advance for any reason.'*

While I admire their honesty, I do not like these comments and I think their terms about moving someone from room to room should be a concern to any prospective resident. No refund of fees paid in advance also sounds unreasonable. What if someone wishes to leave the home because the environment is such that their stay is untenable? Remember – the organisations is saying *no* refund for *any* reason! If challenged, I suspect that the terms would be considered unfair, but has anybody ever challenged them?

> *'Residents can have alcohol in their rooms provided that it is a reasonable amount and that they don't have an alcohol-related problem.'*

What if someone wanted to sit in the lounge and have a drink with a friend, would management insist instead that a person be made to drink alone in their bedroom? Who determines a reasonable amount? Are we talking about a medically diagnosed alcohol-related problem or just the view of the home? Why only in their rooms?

> *'We welcome residents from every cultural, religious or ethnic background. If you require special menus for religious, cultural or dietary needs, our managers will be delighted to discuss your requirements with you. We will also endeavour to ensure you are able to observe and practise your particular religious or cultural beliefs during your stay with us.'*

Other homes did mention some of the above, such as dietary needs associated with religion or culture, but of the 110 brochures received, no other made reference to all of these points, nor in such a positive and thorough way.

DOMICILIARY CARE

> *'Our carers are not cleaners and clients should arrange for cleaning duties to be carried out by other helpers.'*

Later I explain how some domiciliary care providers will not allow care workers to undertake cleaning duties. However, I do think that there are better ways of making this point.

The same company also states they require '40 weeks written notice of cancellation'. On first impressions, I felt sure this was a typing error but in the event it isn't: please let them know 40 weeks in advance if care is no longer required!

Another company stood out for all the right reasons when discussing the care of clients with dementia:

> *'We feel that clients with dementia often have their care decided by what is available and not what is appropriate to their individual need and we are committed to offering solutions to change this.'*

It is annoying when availability of care comes before appropriateness and what I admire about this company is that they are not only acknowledging this fact publicly in their literature, they are seeking to change it.

> *'We never forget that the people to whom we provide a service are not clients or patients but instead are customers and deserve the standards of service and the attention to detail which the relationship demands.'*

This provider recognises that users of care services are 'consumers' and such recognition is vital if organisations are going to offer a good level of customer service.

TERMS AND CONDITIONS

There will be as many sets of terms and conditions as there are care organisations, and as there are well over twenty five thousand providers in England, this is a significant number.

Some terms and conditions will be mundane and others are vital for protection. You must familiarise yourself with the important ones such as:

- levels of insurance cover
- conditions of termination of service

■ notice of termination – which is very important because it is not unheard of for domiciliary care organisations to 'pull out' their service at very short notice or for 'care homes' to ask residents to leave with little time to find alternative accommodation.

A number of domiciliary care companies will permit live-in care workers to be disturbed up to three times during the night. Later in the 'Live-in' section in Chapter 7 I explain why this is not ideal. Such organisations will charge consumers for the wake-up calls and I explain how, on the face of it this will seem like a beneficial term for the consumer, but it can actually be open to abuse.

Some brochures did provide information about how you can register complaints, although several had outdated details in respect of the authorities to contact.

Remember that how you can complain should be a key term and is one with which you must not only familiarise yourself but is one which you are satisfied is adhered to.

OTHER OBSERVATIONS

One organisation stated they were aiming to implement a new training programme in September 2005 yet the brochure was obtained in January 2007. You should never take it for granted that something promised in a brochure has been implemented. Instead check that brochure information is current.

Some companies used misleading pictures. For example, one domiciliary care provider who according to the information clearly provides only care workers has a picture of a nurse in the brochure.

Some care homes recommend trial runs in order that choices about the service are informed, before committing to it. I explain later in greater detail the benefits of doing this, but do not be misled into thinking that, because the care provider offers trials, they must be confident in their wares. The truth is that the NMCS state that trial visits *must* be offered.

Some organisations give assurances that your concerns will be taken seriously, that your complaints will be acted upon and that your assessment of care needs will be undertaken 'free of charge'. However, an assessment is a requirement of the NMCS and therefore *cannot* be charged for.

It was a pleasure to see that a number of companies sent information above and beyond that required. One care home listed a telephone contact for 'Seniorline', which is a free and confidential advice line regarding community care provided by Help the Aged.

Other organisations focused on the quality of their workforce:

'Our care workers are challenged, trained and content.'

It was nice to see the use of the words *care worker* or similar. The term *carer* is, by way of the Carer's (Recognition and Services) Act 1995, reserved for the millions of individuals within England who provide unpaid caring services to relatives or friends. I would therefore place much weight on the term used by a company for their workers because such attention to detail shows respect for those providing care unpaid.

CONCLUSION

Having examined the brochures received from both types of providers I noted the following:

- only a handful had well presented and personalised covering letters
- most had handwritten compliment slips
- others sent nothing personal in response to the enquiry.

There was no clear front-runner between care homes and domiciliary care services regarding the brochures received. However, I feel that domiciliary care providers were unable to rely on photographs of picturesque settings as many of the care homes could. They therefore tended to be a little more descriptive of their services. Very few companies included fees and less than 2 per cent of either of the services included contracts despite the intention of the National Minimum Care Standards that all potential consumers of services be made fully aware of an organisation's terms before buying. Three of the care home brochures did include a resident's charter reflecting the rights of those using the service.

Care services are no different from any other organisation in that they may say one thing in their brochures and do another in reality. But to use the literature of a potential care provider as a starting point is a step in the right direction and some weight should be given to how they present themselves in the first instance.

3

The Role of Professionals

Professionals may play a role in facilitating care choices and I have therefore included those you will most likely have contact with. I have also discussed the support they can offer and have listed them in no particular order of importance.

THE GP

The GP is an important link in the receipt of community services, so a relationship with him or her is especially important. He or she may be the person responsible for referral of an individual's needs to various health bodies such as the district nursing services or physiotherapy departments. I would suggest that the following points are discussed with him or her:

■ you are looking at care options and would like to know what level of support they could offer in the event that a choice to stay at home is made

■ a move into residential or nursing care is likely: will they visit the chosen home?

The GP is also central to medication requirements and as there have been reported rises in the incidence of older people suffering adverse drug reactions (ADRs), all primary care trusts (those employing GPs) are meant to carry out an annual review of medication given to all patients over 75.

If a choice is made to stay at home, I would recommend that the GP undertake a review of medication annually (even if the person cared for is not aged 75 or more) and that a date is set to ensure it becomes a ritual.

If a care home is chosen be sure that the home has a policy of annual review of medication, again regardless of age.

It would be advisable to check with a doctor *prior* to taking unprescribed medicines, no matter how innocent the medicine may seem, and even if the remedy was previously taken. Health will change with age or illness and reactions to over-the-counter medicines may differ as a person's health needs change, not only as they become older.

DISTRICT NURSES

If some sort of nursing service is required but entering a nursing home is not a preference, district nursing services can provide excellent levels of support at home.

Should an individual require district nursing services, contact the GP surgery and ask to be transferred to the nursing team. If, on speaking with you, the nurse agrees a service is required, they will usually speak with the doctor to arrange this.

Training provided by district nurses

District nurses can deliver various services such as wound dressing and incontinence management, and they may even be willing to train care workers to undertake basic tasks. When effectively managed, such services can maximise independence and provide greater flexibility to a daily routine, such as enabling the cared-for person to go on holiday with a trained care worker.

There is also no legal reason why nurses cannot train care workers to undertake more complex procedures – such as administering suppositories – but views on this will differ with various local authorities depending on the district nursing team's own internal policy.

If you decide to employ a private care worker, any agreement for training by the nurses is between the person employing the worker, the worker, the nurse and any insurance companies providing cover.

Agreement to training

When workers are supplied by a domiciliary care organisation providing a full 'service' then it is *vital* to seek provider agreement *before* district nurses provide training of any type. This is because not all domiciliary care companies will allow their care workers to undertake tasks that are nursing-related, and those who do may hold views on the level of task based on guidance from their insurers or any governing bodies. A domiciliary organisation acting solely as an agent introducing workers will not have control over issues such as training. You will instead need to deal with the situation as per privately employing. For this reason it is important to be clear on the exact legal relationship you have with your care provider.

Confirmation of training

Where a care organisation allows workers to be trained by a third party it is good practice that they request written confirmation of that training. If there is nothing in writing, problems could arise. With this in mind, I would recommend that *all* care worker training be confirmed in writing, no matter how basic the task and regardless of who supplies the worker. This is because unless the district nursing team are willing to put in writing that they have carried out training and unless they are *confident* a worker is *competent* to undertake the tasks delegated to them, I would be concerned as to who would be held responsible in the event of something medically going wrong.

Medical responsibility

Anyone receiving district nursing care should be afforded some protection in that all qualified nurses must adhere to the NMC (Nursing and Midwifery Council) Code of Professional Conduct. As of August 2007, the code states:

> **4.6** You may be expected to delegate care delivery to others who are not registered nurses or midwives. Such delegation must not compromise existing care but must be directed to meeting the needs and serving the interests of patients and clients. You remain accountable for the appropriateness of the delegation, for ensuring that the person who does the work is able to do it and that adequate supervision or support is provided.

If a district nurse has delegated a task, ultimately the medical responsibility will remain with them. Yet, without a clear record of who provided the training and when, it could be hard to prove *which* nurse delegated a task. This is especially true if a surgery has a high turnover of district nurses or they use temporary workers, so the most prudent approach would be to clarify matters from the outset. This is not about blame but about ensuring that the person in receipt of care is protected.

Time between visits

There should also be a time limit between visits by the district nurse that should not be exceeded. There may be times when a nurse will need to monitor the progress of a condition and evaluate delegated tasks. This will minimise the chances of a worker doing anything that could exacerbate a particular condition. Don't be afraid to make it clear that you have an expectation in respect of such monitoring or it might not happen.

Training replacement care workers

If a trained care worker is leaving their position then discourage cascaded training between the existing worker and replacements. Instead request that any training originally provided by a district nurse is again provided by them for subsequent workers.

> **REMEMBER**
> Make no apologies for caution in respect of training because without care workers, district nurses would need to provide a more frequent service.

Specialist care

District nurses can also assist in calling in more specialised professionals such as Macmillan nurses to provide palliative care for those with a terminal condition.

OCCUPATIONAL THERAPISTS

An occupational therapist (OT) may be required if someone at home is undertaking rehabilitation or if their condition is such that physically they are less able and require aids or adaptations.

An OT will provide or advise on the purchase of equipment such as hoists, walking frames, grab rails, stair lifts and profiler electric beds, or indeed any equipment aimed at the promotion of physical independence and well-being. Ask the OT for advice on equipment hire and purchase but if they are unable to point you in the right direction then the Red Cross may be able to help or suggest suppliers.

In some cases, the OT can make the difference between an individual's only choice being to move into a residential facility because the home environment is unsuitable or, with the help of specialist equipment, that choice being extended to receipt of services at home.

PHYSIOTHERAPISTS

A physiotherapist (often abbreviated simply to 'physio') is frequently fundamental for effective physical rehabilitation and may be involved at home or within a residential environment.

As with nursing services, if a physio trains a care worker or third party then this should be confirmed in writing and where possible pictorial information should be provided. If at all practical it would be ideal to make a video diary of an exercise session by simply videoing the physio undertaking the exercises. This way, anyone helping with exercises in the absence of the physio can refer to the tape to refresh their memory. I make this suggestion because physiotherapists are highly qualified individuals who train both academically and physically for many years to perfect their skills.

Someone trained for a short period and left to the task of undertaking exercises has the potential to cause problems if they can't recall the advice they were given clearly.

> **IT'S A FACT**
> Poorly performed exercises can be more damaging than no exercise at all.

> **Note**
> It is important to gain permission from the physio to video an exercise session.

A good physio will be realistic about the chances of a complete return to physical independence and will discuss limitations (if indeed there are any) based on the current state of health.

Physios are often provided by community services such as a GP, but the wait to see one can be lengthy. Once in receipt of a service, time allocated can be short such as a one-off visit or a set number of hours.

A lot will depend on where the physio comes from, their budget, the patient's age and the chances of rehabilitation. Although they can be hard to source, there is scope to employ a physio privately.

Even if an individual lives in a care home setting, if it is required some physiotherapy should be given. Who should pay for it will depend on the circumstances, but if in doubt you should contact your GP or Social Services and ask for advice.

DENTISTS, OPTICIANS AND AUDIOLOGISTS

Even if a person can't go out, don't neglect their oral, visual or audio health. Many dentists, opticians and audiologists will provide a domiciliary service.

If required at home, then contact the relevant professional associations to enquire about domiciliary services in the area. If a person is in a care home, then ask the home manager whether they can arrange services.

CHIROPODISTS

Whatever the care setting, I would discourage care workers from cutting toe nails, especially if a person suffers from diabetes. This is because a chiropodist can detect problems with circulation and they are meticulous about not damaging the toes of those with such a condition.

> **HIGH PRIORITY**
> Blunders with foot care for those suffering from diabetes can lead to complications, which at the most extreme could result in the amputation of toes.

If in a residential or nursing home, ask about the home's policy on cutting of finger and toe nails so that arrangements can be made to access these services.

AROMATHERAPISTS

Many of us are now recognising the benefits of aromatherapy as an alternative to chemical pain relief as well as for pure relaxation.

I am a great advocate of doing anything that suits one's belief and budget, but would strongly advise against using an aromatherapist who is not registered with a reliable and recognised association.

This is because, despite its 'natural' approach and the harmless image that aromatherapy conjures up, there are many aromatherapy oils that must not be used in conjunction with others. Care must also be taken when a person suffers from certain medical conditions, is pregnant or uses particular medications. Some oils would not be suitable for children.

A qualified and registered individual will be aware of the importance of discussing issues such as medication as well as general health before offering any type of aromatherapy treatment.

4

Care Choices

Having explored ways of accessing services and the type of professionals available to support choices, it is now time to consider the type of care that is right for the situation you are planning.

There are factors that will influence the care choices but regardless of whether a care home or domiciliary care is eventually chosen, some general points about the services will be shared. So in this chapter I cover shared points and then in subsequent chapters I go on to separate each category of care service. I list the pros and cons relevant to the individual services in order to encourage you to address those points realistically and thoroughly.

Having done so, you can then make a fully-informed decision as to whether domiciliary care is a viable option or if a care home is the only way forward.

WHAT ARE THE OPTIONS?

Living-in a *care home* environment would mean an individual would be supervised and monitored and the daily routine would be predetermined (to a degree) by those in charge of the establishment. There would probably be little to worry about logistically.

Receiving *domiciliary care* would mean that everything associated with running a home, such as paying bills, would still need to be dealt with, but with an added consideration – that of the welfare of care workers.

> **WHAT DO YOU THINK?**
> Would being in a care home mean one *loses* **control, or will remaining in one's own home mean** *retaining full* **control? We will take a closer look at this and other issues.**

CONTROL

Receiving a care service requires compromise on the part of the consumer whatever the setting and regardless of how flexible a service is. With ever-evolving employment laws and human rights issues, the rights of the consumers of care as well as care workers must be continually addressed and balanced. Such compromise is rarely more apparent than when we are giving consideration to issues of control.

Few of us like to feel out of control whatever our age, but we have to be realistic about the limitations faced by providers of services. If I did not encourage consideration of this fact I would be guilty of selling an *unrealistic* or *ideal* care setup. This is something far too many consumers of care services are sold daily.

So will there be a loss of control in a care home setting?

To a degree, care homes *can* (and the good ones *will*) seek to involve their consumers in making meaningful choices, but realistically they can do this only to a point.

Any establishment of significant size, if it is to run smoothly, must be allowed to determine routine and retain control. So yes, there would inevitably be a certain degree of loss of control.

Some homes will be better equipped to be flexible to consumers' needs and preferences, but none the less *all care homes will have their limitations*. For example, it would be virtually impossible for the chef of a 50-bedded care establishment to ask every individual resident what they would like for lunch on the day and respond to those requests, as he might receive 50 different orders. To enable residents to feel involved and have a certain amount of choice, chef will run his kitchen as one would run a kitchen in a restaurant, by having a menu, thus *controlling and limiting choices to a manageable size*. This makes good sense, but that is not to say that homes would not be responsive if someone really didn't like what was on the menu. In any case, they must cater for special diets and tastes, but an alternative would probably have to be requested.

Even though care homes must offer choices, those choices will undoubtedly be limited and influenced by the establishment. The same principle will apply when deciding:

- meal times (although we have demonstrated in the section on brochures that some homes manage to let individuals eat whenever they wish)

- colour schemes around the home (other than perhaps in one's own bedroom)

- entertainment services that may be bought into the home (which would have to appeal to the majority) and

- who the home employs.

Modern and progressive care homes would be responsive to minority requirements and good homes will run residents' meetings and have methods of evaluation in place in order to gain the opinion of those using the service.

> **YOU SHOULD NOTE**
>
> For meetings or evaluation processes to be beneficial, they must:
>
> ■ be purposeful – not just merely a process to impress inspectors
> ■ have minutes that can be seen by any interested party – all purposeful meetings would have minutes
> ■ have evidence that shows evaluation methods are valid.

And what control can domiciliary care have?

A contentious control issue affecting this type of service is that of bedtime. This issue is when the balance of control between care provider/worker and consumer can become the most strained.

If care is delivered by a 'service provider' (this is a company who employs their staff and provides a full service), then the provider organisation will have health and safety issues that need to be considered. This will have a knock-on effect on the level of influence a consumer can have regarding the delivery of their care.

The bedtime example reflects this well because there will be times when an individual may not want to go to bed until midnight, but the service provider is unwilling to allow workers to provide care after 10 p.m. for reasons of safety. Such situations can cause a sense of loss of control.

If employing a worker 'privately' or through an organisation solely introducing care workers, then more flexibility with bedtime may be possible, because some private workers (but not all) may be happy to work late. Experience tells me though that it is unlikely that anyone will retain care workers for any length of time if they are asking for very late bedtime calls (e.g. 11.30 p.m.) and are then asking the same care worker for early morning calls (e.g. 7 a.m.) because under such circumstances workers will become tired.

A feeling of loss over the ultimate control of bedtime routines is understandable, but it reinforces the fact that compromise is inevitable when in receipt of care services.

There are combinations of care that can cater for the needs of individuals who like to go to bed late and rise early in the morning. This point will be discussed in greater detail in Chapter 7 on domiciliary care but it must be said that, as with most 'alternatives', it will come at a premium and if domiciliary care is funded by the local authority, then limitations on the level of service may be imposed due to cost, again taking away the individual's ultimate control.

EMPLOYMENT

Successful care services are built on reliable and trained care workers, administration and management teams. The difficulty is that certain areas of England suffer staff shortages and this affects all types of care organisations.

Whatever our age, most of us like continuity, and providers should always endeavour to provide this. But staff shortages can cause problems, especially for *domiciliary care organisations*. Staffing is one of their greatest challenges.

An advantage of a *care home* setting is that they will probably have several care staff with whom residents feel comfortable. If one worker is on holiday or absent through sickness, they will still have others to whom they can easily relate. This is not something that is always readily available with domiciliary care.

What type of workers might a care service employ?

Don't make the assumption that all care staff will be very experienced care givers, even in nursing homes, because everyone has to start somewhere. It is unlikely that any provider of care, even if they only ever use workers with previous experience, will always be able to supply staff with knowledge of every medical condition.

Given the potential for staff shortages, it would be impossible for care providers to dismiss those willing to undertake the work of caring, just because they lack previous or specific condition-related experience. If they did, then there would be a large proportion of very good services unable to operate.

Employers can teach individuals to provide practical care by giving them good quality training, but you can't *teach* someone to be kind and caring.

Individuals attracted to the care profession are invaluable. Every good applicant with the right qualities as a person should be considered regardless of previous experience, *but only* if the employer provides quality training.

WHAT IS NOT QUALITY TRAINING?

- It is *not* sitting trainees in front of a video recorder and a TV set and *calling* it training!
- It is *not* sending trainees to a rival organisation to gain training and then employing them.
- It is *not* sitting them in a room and talking at them.

QUALITY TRAINING WILL INCLUDE

- Giving trainees physical tasks to undertake and physically assessing their ability.
- Giving trainees training specific to the organisation employing them in order that policy and procedure is appropriate.
- Giving trainees an opportunity to be involved in tasks such as role play.

What makes a good care worker?

There are many important factors that make a good care worker, and these include (but are not limited to):

- being kind and caring
- being flexible
- being patient
- being understanding
- having empathy
- showing commitment
- being reliable
- being friendly and personable.

If employers choose their workers wisely, they will know that the good ones always try to improve the lives of others and enjoy the rewarding feeling it gives them. Care workers deserve to be paid as much as any profession and my experience is that few of them do it *just* for the money. They do it because they enjoy helping people to live happy, fulfilled lives.

What makes care workers dissatisfied?

Yet, even those with a halo can be pushed to their limits. I have met care workers who, for a thousand pounds per week, would still refuse to continue working for an employer or consumer of a service if they felt they were not treating them well.

Whatever the care setting, the types of things that might upset care workers and make them feel undervalued are:

- verbal or physical abuse (unless the individual receiving the care has a medical condition that means their behaviour is impaired and workers are aware of this prior to accepting the position)
- being treated as subservient
- being asked to undertake unrealistic amounts of domestic chores
- being belittled in any way
- being expected to work very long and erratic hours
- no consideration being given to their needs and feelings
- prejudice.

You must aim to buy into services that treat their staff with respect and support them well. If you are privately employing, be mindful of these points. After all, it is the recipient of the care who will suffer if there is tension in an environment where workers feel unsettled or undervalued.

Care workers from overseas

Whether experienced or not, some care organisations are left with little option but to employ care workers from overseas to bridge the workforce shortage gap – which brings me onto my next subject.

PREJUDICE, OR ISSUES OF COMPATIBILITY?

I'm sure that you will agree that prejudice of any kind does not belong in a civilised society.

Care organisations are legally bound to employ people who are capable of doing a good job whatever their colour, size, gender, sexuality or otherwise. But making a choice about who we would want to care for us is not as straightforward as it seems.

Compatibility

We normally choose our friends based on personal preferences and shared experiences of life. Such an approach maximises our chances of compatibility and of formulating long-term and meaningful relationships.

We cannot use the same approach when choosing a care home setting. There are too many residents and care staff to determine whether an individual will get along with everyone, but the law of averages says that there will be some compatible associations. However, with domiciliary care, it is easier to achieve a match between a worker and the needs and preferences of a consumer because of the one-on-one nature of the service (such compatibility is essential in a domiciliary setting). However, this can happen only if time is afforded to match the care worker to the consumer based on the needs and preferences of each of them.

For example, it would be pointless if a user of a service is a smoker who requires live-in care and a domiciliary company sends an anti-smoking care worker. This would be a recipe for disaster, as would their supplying a worker who hates dogs when the cared for individual has three.

Concerns about potential compatibility with a care worker should be discussed with the service provider/agency.

If faced with uncertainty about compatibility with a potential worker, or the cared for individual dislikes a worker already *in situ*, be sure to base views on facts and don't make comments about their colour, race, size, sexuality, etc. to the provider organisation. Even if unintentional, any reference to such factors *may* sound like prejudice.

Racism

Any reputable company will respect real and genuine issues raised regarding compatibility as differences might conflict not only with the cared for person's happiness, but with that of the care worker. But if a consumer displays blatant behaviour that indicates racism, it would not be unusual for an organisation to refuse to continue providing care although this would depend upon their legal position, for example if they employ the care workers or merely introduce them.

Gender

Experience tells me that many people do not have an issue with the sex of their care workers, but consumers do have a right to *refuse* to accept care of an intimate and personal nature from a care worker of the opposite sex if to do so would make them feel uncomfortable. If a care provider tries to force a consumer to accept direct care (such as being washed or taken to the bathroom) from a worker of the opposite sex, regardless of the care setting – then this is not acceptable. If they claim that they cannot discriminate against workers and must employ all genders – then this is accurate. However, employing workers and supplying them are two different things. They cannot be accused of discrimination if on employing workers there is a 'genuine vocational qualification', for example where a female consumer does not wish to receive direct care from a male care worker that may limit some of their duties.

Language

Finally, although care providers face problems and staff shortages, it is not acceptable for them to employ care workers who are not able to speak English to an understandable level (an accent is acceptable, but it is understanding that is vital) and appropriate to the person for whom they provide the care. Such a lack of basic communication could prove dangerous. This is, of course, unless a service is one specifically aimed at French or Hindi speakers, for example, when these would be the languages of primary importance.

LEGAL PROTECTION

If a consumer tries to dissuade care workers from following the care provider's health and safety advice, for example a consumer does not want to be hoisted or use equipment to aid in their transfers, despite agreeing with the provider of the service, that they may do so, *and* the consumer persuades a care worker to lift them (when nobody is looking) and that worker hurts themselves, *then* it is worth noting that a consumer could be deemed just as liable as the care worker or the care company.

If, during the planning of care, a consumer is *not in agreement* with a risk assessment or a subsequent action plan, then concerns must be discussed and a way forward found. Do not just ignore what is agreed.

REMEMBER

Health and safety laws are there to protect all concerned – especially consumers of care.

FAMILIARITY BREEDS CONTEMPT

It is natural that once people become better acquainted, open discussions may be had on a variety of subjects such as families and lifestyle. But problems can occur once care workers get to know a person better, because whatever the care setting, professional boundaries can often be challenged. The minimum care standards do set some guidance on the subject and specify the line over which care workers should not cross in terms of accepting gifts for example. Many subjects can be deemed inappropriate for care workers to discuss with a consumer of services, and these include:

- money worries
- marital problems
- intimate health problems
- social issues such as 'a member of their family has been sent to prison'.

Some workers may misread the signs and think that politeness in listening is an open invitation of a shoulder for them to cry on and some people may have no problem listening to or discussing with a care worker their woes. Even if a consumer is happy listening to a care worker's problems I would encourage them to reconsider their position. What if it is money a worker is concerned about? Does anyone really want to offer a care worker a loan, or worse still, be asked to help financially?

If care workers are asking too many questions about a consumer's life, or giving too much information about theirs, then this must either be discussed with them (if one feels comfortable to do so) or alternatively a senior staff member or management should be approached.

If a care worker asks to borrow money or possessions, then this must be reported to the management of the service immediately.

In the event that it is management crossing the boundaries such as asking for a loan, then concerns must be reported to the CSCI, as such behaviour is highly inappropriate whatever the position of the offender.

Although it is a hard balance to strike, it is possible to have a friendly and meaningful relationship with care workers and managers while still retaining professional boundaries.

DISSATISFACTION WITH SERVICE

If at any time dissatisfaction with a care company is felt and the matter is a fairly simple one, then regardless of how difficult it might be to do so, management must be spoken with directly, not via care workers as they are rarely in a position to change anything. It is not fair to involve care workers with daily gripes as they may feel torn between the consumer and their employer. If workers feel the desire to complain to consumers about their employment, they should be encouraged to talk to management directly.

If the dissatisfaction is of a more serious nature, then consumers must use the care provider's complaints procedure to find a resolution to the problem. I do accept that there are sensitive issues when it might be appropriate to include a care worker, but this should only be if there are genuine concerns that, should the management of a service be involved, there would be a fear of reprisal, *and only* in the unlikely event that there is no alternative professional third party available in whom one can confide, such as the CSCI or Social Services.

A common complaint that consumers make to care workers is the cost of the service. Likewise, complaints from care workers to consumers are usually pay related. Such discussions will breed unrest for all concerned and the care provider must have an opportunity to explain what the difference between the care worker's salary and the cost of the fees covers. Consumers may be satisfied with the explanation or may not, yet one thing is guaranteed – complaining between consumer and care worker won't change a thing. However, discussing it with the care provider just might!

If there is a problem with a care worker, then it is nearly always best to speak directly to the care provider, but again it will depend on the relationship with the worker and the nature of the issue. Due to the scope for complexity on this subject, my suggestions cannot possibly be exhaustive.

5

Does Abuse *Really* Happen?

BACKGROUND TO ABUSE

Just before we look in detail at available care choices and begin planning the most suitable package of care, I want to encourage you to look at the issue of abuse of vulnerable adults. Child protection awareness is much higher than adult protection awareness. There will be many of you who are unaware of the scope of the problem of adult abuse, other than what you have been exposed to within the media.

This can be a controversial subject and while I do not wish to add to the burden of fear already experienced by some people, I want to provide you with some facts in order that you are aware of *what abuse is* and *how it might affect those receiving care*. This will enable you to maximise your chances of protecting yourself or the person for whom you are arranging the service.

Abuse is not necessarily being 'beaten up by the owner of a care home' – in many cases it is far more subtle. Poor practice and institutional abuse can occur and abusive behaviour does not need to be intentional to be damaging.

Example

Budock Hospital in Cornwall provided services for adults with learning disabilities. Following a joint investigation at the Cornwall Partnership NHS trust by the CSCI and the Health Inspectorate in March 2007, information was posted on the CSCI website in relation to the nature of the abuse found to be occurring within that care setting. The trust's own investigations felt that users of the service had had to endure years of abusive practices and some had suffered real injury as a result.

The report following the investigation included these statements:

> *Despite the development of numerous action plans, underlying problems have never been addressed and poor practice has become ingrained within the management of learning disability services and the provision of care.*

> *Our investigation found that institutional abuse was widespread...*

> *More than two-thirds of the sites we visited placed unacceptable restrictions on people living there.*

> *During the investigation, the Healthcare Commission and CSCI referred 40 individuals under the procedures for the protection of vulnerable adults, as set out in the No Secrets guidance, relating to these and other practices.*

Abuse is a difficult subject to address, but I believe that I have a duty to heighten awareness as it is not easy to identify something if it is not understood. If a person receiving care thinks that abuse is not common, they may feel to blame if they are targeted. As a consequence they may be embarrassed and not wish to report abuse regardless of any efforts to show them how they can.

SO WHAT IS ABUSE AND HOW CAN YOU RECOGNISE IT?

Below are two definitions of abuse although there will be others:

Elder abuse is a single or repeated act, or lack of appropriate action occurring within any relationship where there is an expectation of trust, that causes harm or distress to an older person. (Action on Elder Abuse)

Abuse is a violation of individuals' human and civil rights by any other person or persons. (No Secrets)

It has been suggested by the Law Commission that:

Harm should be taken to include not only ill-treatment (including sexual abuse and forms of ill-treatment which are not physical), but also the impairment of, or an avoidable deterioration in, physical or mental health; and the impairment of physical, intellectual, emotional, social or behavioural development. (Taken from Camden Adult Protection Procedure)

Abuse can be inflicted by:

- *a third party – unknown*
- *a third party – known*
- *self-inflicted abuse (as distinct from self-neglect or substance abuse)*
- *other vulnerable adults who are care consumers*

■ *people who deliberately form a relationship with a vulnerable person in order to exploit them.*

and take place within both personal and professional relationships. (Taken from Camden Adult Protection Procedure.)

CATEGORIES OF ABUSE

For the purposes of this chapter I classify eight categories of abuse:

■ **Physical** – can include hitting, slapping, pushing, kicking.
■ **Institutional** – can include inappropriate restraint, misuse of medication.
■ **Sexual** – can include rape, sexual assault.
■ **Psychological/emotional** – can include humiliation, threats, harassment, coercion, blaming.
■ **Sectarian** – can include exposure to inappropriate songs and banners.
■ **Financial** – can include theft, misuse of property, finances or benefits.
■ **Neglect** – can include withholding necessities of life, care needs.
■ **Discrimination** – can include racism, sexism, slurs, discrimination based upon disabilities.

SYMPTOMS AND INDICATORS

Physical abuse

Indicators that a vulnerable adult might be *physically* abused (intentionally or unintentionally) could include:

■ bruises for which there is no explanation of how they occurred

- injuries inconsistent with explanations of how they occurred
- clusters of injuries
- burns and scalds of any description including cigarette burns
- unintentional weight loss
- dehydration
- nervous/fearful watchfulness
- fear of physical contact.

Institutional abuse

Indicators that a vulnerable adult might be subjected to *institutional* abuse (intentionally or unintentionally) could include:

- the adult being over-medicated – often used to control behaviour to suit the social environment rather than in the best interest of the vulnerable adult
- the adult being denied appropriate levels of medication/pain control
- the use of inappropriate restraint.

Sexual abuse

Indicators that a vulnerable adult might be being subjected to *sexual* abuse could include:

- the adult displaying signs of soreness/pain or unexplained rashes in the genital areas
- stained/bloodstained underclothes
- unexplained bruises on their inner thighs and buttocks
- unexplained discomfort when sitting or walking
- sexually transmitted diseases when not known to be sexually active
- pregnancy when not known to be sexually active.

Psychological/emotional abuse

Indicators that a vulnerable adult might be subjected to *psychological/emotional* abuse (intentionally or unintentionally) could include:

- the adult displaying unwarranted fear of people and places not associated with their medical condition
- bed-wetting when incontinence has not been initially diagnosed
- a distrust of people
- depression not associated with their medical condition
- emotional withdrawal
- high levels of anxiety.

Sectarian abuse

Indicators that a vulnerable adult is being subjected to *sectarian* abuse (intentionally or unintentionally) could include witnessing:

- an adult being exposed to flags, emblems and symbols deemed inappropriate or offensive to their beliefs
- a distrust/fearfulness of ministers of religion
- slurs and offensive remarks regarding their religious beliefs.

Financial abuse

Indicators that a vulnerable adult might be being subjected to *financial* abuse could include:

- sudden loss of cash or earnings
- inability to afford the basic service when the person is known to have financial means
- theft of personal property
- missing personal property (jewellery, cash, etc.)

- power of attorney obtained illegally
- third party cashing benefits which do not appear to benefit client
- fraud involving wills, property and other assets.

Neglect

Indicators that a vulnerable adult might be being subjected to *neglect* (intentionally or unintentionally) could include:

- unauthorised withdrawal of basic services
- persistent weight loss/emaciation/malnutrition
- untreated bedsores, ulcers and other skin conditions
- poor personal care
- inadequate/inappropriate bedding/clothing
- third party cashing benefits which do not appear to benefit client.

Discrimination

Indicators that a vulnerable adult is being subjected to *discrimination* (intentionally or unintentionally) could include witnessing:

- evidence of racism
- evidence of sexism
- evidence of ageism
- slurs and offensive remarks regarding ethnic origin, religion, culture, sex and age
- discriminatory practices based upon the person's disabilities.

INVESTIGATIONS INTO ABUSE

I have been involved in seven cases of investigation of abuse by domiciliary care workers over a nine-year period, only one of which was found to be intentional – which of course is one too many. But on analysis of these cases there were always best practice issues to be addressed, lessons learnt and practices improved.

Comic Relief and the Department of Health commissioned an investigation into the true extent of abuse and neglect suffered by older people. The research provides the first nationally representative prevalence estimates regarding mistreatment of older people in the UK.

The report found the following.

- 2.6 per cent of people aged 66 and over living in private households (including sheltered housing) reported that they had experienced mistreatment involving a family member, friend or care worker during the past year.

- This equates to about 227,000 aged 66 or over, or around 1 in 40 of the older population.

- When the one-year prevalence of mistreatment was broadened to include incidents involving neighbours and acquaintances, the figures rose from 2.6 per cent to 4.0 per cent – meaning 342,400 older people being subjected to some form of mistreatment.

- The predominant type of mistreatment reported was neglect (1.1 per cent), followed by financial abuse (0.7 per cent), psychological and physical abuse was similar (both 0.4 per cent), and sexual abuse (reported cases were of harassment) was the least prevalent at (0.2 per cent).

- Women were more likely to say that they had experienced mistreatment than men: 3.8 per cent of women and 1.1 per cent of men.

- Mistreatment in the past year varied significantly by marital status, and increased with declining health, status, depression and loneliness.

- Fifty-one per cent of mistreatment in the past year involved a spouse/partner, 49 per cent another family member, 13 per cent a care worker and 5 per cent a close friend. (Respondents could mention more than one person.)

The data did not take into account any other category of adults – it concerned solely older people – and included only five categories of abuse: neglect, financial, psychological, physical and sexual.

It is important that you find a care provider who will take allegations of abuse seriously *whatever age the person receiving the service*.

You should find it reassuring to know that there is government guidance specifically for the investigation of allegations of abuse and all regulated services must follow this guidance, which needs to be reflected within their own policy and procedures. What you need to be certain of before buying into a service is: 'Does the care provider you are researching follow that guidance?'

HOW SHOULD A CARE PROVIDER HANDLE ALLEGATIONS OF ABUSE?

- If it is brought to the attention of a care provider that an employee has been behaving in an abusive manner, the provider's first priority must be towards the person being cared for.

- Care workers must be allowed to give their version of events and protection must also be afforded the accused as justice states a person is innocent until proven guilty.

- The organisation should have policies and procedures that must be followed in order that investigations are not compromised. You must satisfy yourself that any provider organisation has robust policy, reflective of a set of procedures that are considerate of *all parties*.

- In the event that accusations are true, there must not be scope for a vulnerable person to be further abused.

- All allegations must be investigated within a certain timeframe and the vulnerable person (or their representative) should be kept informed of progress.

- Regular updates should be provided at an appropriate level without jeopardising the investigation by giving too much information away. This is not always an easy task for organisations but they have a duty to face such challenges and find solutions for the protection of all involved.

- Care providers and their workers should be trained in reporting and investigating allegations of abuse. Local councils take the matter very seriously and provide free or low-cost courses to care providers on this subject. Adult abuse training should be updated regularly (the NMCS states at least every two years) and you must satisfy yourself that providers are conversant and trained.

- If a care worker is found guilty of abuse, they should be taken through the disciplinary process and discharged from their position. Care providers then have a duty to refer abusive workers to the Protection of Vulnerable Adults (POVA) list for consideration for inclusion by the Secretary of State. Once a case has been considered, and if the Secretary of State feels it is warranted, the individual's name will be logged on the list until it is deemed appropriate to remove it, during which time they will be banned for a period of time from working within a care setting.

- This list must be checked, by law, as part of the recruitment process by all care providers and, in the event of a worker being listed, they should *not* be employed. While the list is a very positive deterrent to abuse – a negative of the process is that the success is reliant on the competence of the care provider to effectively handle the process of investigation and to make a referral.

The Protection of Vulnerable Adults list

The DoH has provided the following details of the number of individuals included on the POVA list as at 30 March 2007:

- 6,352 people had been referred to the POVA list of which
- 1,009 people are confirmed on it and
- 1,300 people are provisionally listed.

This means that a total of 2,309 people are prevented from working in regulated social care settings. In the same period 3,927 cases were closed as they did not meet the criteria for the scheme to list them.

Future plans

There are future plans to replace the current list under the Safeguarding Vulnerable Groups legislation and the responsibility for barring members of the workforce will transfer from the minister to an independent barring board. I suspect that such a change will not lessen the need for care providers to be alert and responsive to allegations and to refer individuals for inclusion.

Approach to investigating allegations of abuse

Unfortunately some care providers might be apprehensive over instigating adult abuse investigations for many reasons. They may fear that, in the event of a worker being found guilty, it will reflect badly on their care services. I believe that an open and honest approach to the matter can only reflect positively on organisations, unless a care provider has poor recruitment practices in which case they should rightly be concerned that they have in some way contributed to a problem.

Anyone who intends employing a care worker privately will not automatically have access to the banned workforce list. I give further details in Chapter 8 on measures you can take to minimise the risks of employing an abusive individual.

IMPORTANT

If you or someone you know is suffering abuse call the Action on Elder abuse response helpline on 0808 8088141 or contact your local Social Services department to seek advice on the correct course of action.

6

Care Homes

We will now look in detail at the care options available and find out more about what each has to offer.

As previously mentioned, I cover residential and nursing care homes (including respite and rehabilitation) within this section.

I provide a general overview of the different types of homes as well as the pros and cons of each. I encourage you to question whether any of the care home options are right for you or the individual on behalf of whom you are making enquiries.

I suspect you will already be formulating a view of the preferred type of care based on the topics we have so far covered. These topics include how professionals can support choices and (probably more so) the issues we addressed in Chapter 4. Do keep an open mind until you have looked at all feasible options.

RESIDENTIAL HOMES

As a general rule, homes that offer purely residential care facilities tend to cost less than nursing homes. The main difference is that residential homes are not normally equipped with devices such as mechanical lifting aids, and workers need not be as qualified as those in nursing homes. This type of care service will not usually be registered to care for any consumer with high levels of medical or physical need.

Residential care homes are therefore primarily designed to provide a safe and social environment for the more able individual such as active older people and those with learning disabilities as apposed to physical limitations. However, problems can arise if a person becomes physically dependent.

What happens if a person's health deteriorates?

Having settled into a residential home, a person may need to be moved to a nursing home if their health deteriorates, as many residential settings simply do not have adequate facilities or appropriately trained staff to deal with a decline in health or physical well-being. And even if a residential home was willing to care for a more dependent individual, their conditions of registration with the CSCI may prohibit this.

Such a move could be distressing for the individual, their family and friends. In the event that the consumer is 'self-funding', it could also have a negative impact on their financial arrangements.

Unfortunately few of us have a crystal ball and so in the absence of being able to see into the future, planning care may involve some guesstimating as to how a person's health will be a few years down the road.

If it is already known that a person has a condition likely to cause deterioration of either their physical or mental capacity, then be aware that a move to another establishment at some point in the future is possible if a residential care home is the initial choice of care service.

If care is being funded by the local authority, there would be a strong argument for requesting that such an individual not be placed into a residential care home (if one is being considered) because, if they are known to have a degenerative condition, a residential home is unlikely to be able to accommodate their needs indefinitely.

Dual registration homes

One compromise is to find an establishment that has dual registration. Such a home has a limited number of beds for more able individuals. In the event of a consumer's physical health deteriorating, then a move to one of the nursing beds to receive a higher level of care will be the only move necessary.

The cost of a residential bed in a dual registered home is likely to be slightly higher than a purpose-run residential one, but the benefits do outweigh the slightly higher associated costs.

Type of care staff

In terms of size, residential care homes often have smaller numbers of consumers and consequently smaller numbers of care staff. This can mean that residential homes have a feeling of 'homeliness' which is very appealing.

As residential care homes are not intended for the nursing of individuals, the qualifications of residential care staff tend to be lower than those of staff in nursing homes. Those running residential establishments are usually more experienced care workers who have moved their way into management. This said, there are minimum requirements regarding the qualifications of managers, but time is permitted to enable managers to attain those qualifications.

Short-term nursing care

In the event that a person requires some form of nursing in the short term that does not warrant hospitalisation, then it is unlikely that they would be asked to move from a residential care home to a nursing facility. But when planning care you will need to be satisfied that any temporary arrangements in respect of nursing care provided within a residential setting are undertaken by an individual *suitably qualified* to meet that need; otherwise request that the services of a *district nurse* are enlisted.

Advantages of residential care

- The individual is in a safe environment with 24-hour supervision.

- Well-run establishments will have a productive programme of internal and external activities.

- The smaller size of residential facilities can sometimes make them feel friendlier and more like home than nursing establishments.

- Routines will often be more flexible than within larger establishments.

- Associated costs are less than a nursing home.

Disadvantages of residential care

- For some individuals, the move from their own home is in itself a disadvantage.

- There is the potential for a further move if health declines.

Important points to address when considering residential care as an option

- Does the individual have a medical condition that is likely to mean decreased ability physically within the foreseeable future?

- Is the condition likely to deteriorate quickly?

- Is the condition unpredictable?

- Is the condition terminal?

If you have answered yes to any of the above it is important that, if considering residential care, you discuss the medical condition in greater detail with the residential care home. This is so that you can be sure that this is the correct care provision in the long term.

All of these issues will become apparent when the home undertakes a thorough assessment of care needs, but it is better to pre-empt them so as not to waste valuable planning time by looking at care options that are simply not viable.

NURSING HOMES

Nursing homes can accommodate a wide range of people with a number of conditions and are designed to provide a safe and social environment for the more dependent individual.

All nursing homes should have adequate equipment, qualifications and sufficient numbers of trained staff to provide a good service to any category of consumer for whom they are registered to care.

If you are choosing a nursing home, problems later on will be minimised if physical dependency becomes greater than at the time of admission as the home is likely to be able to care for individuals indefinitely. However, there are always exceptions. For example, a nursing home may be chosen which does not have registration to care for people with dementia. If a consumer develops this condition, they would have to be moved to a more specialised home. You can really only *try* to limit the chances of a move being necessary.

One way to do this is to try to find an establishment that has registration for most categories of care. Then, with the exception of hospitalisation being required for more serious health problems, you can be fairly confident that a nursing home will remain home for the duration of a consumer's life.

Unlike many residential homes, nursing homes often have a large number of consumers and 40–50 bedded establishments are not unusual.

Due to the fact that these homes are intended for residents who require nursing, the staff complement should always include at least one qualified nurse at all times (and often more), depending on the size of the home.

Advantages to this type of care

- It is a 24-hour medically supervised environment.

- Well-run establishments will have a productive programme of internal and external activities.

- It is less likely that an individual will be moved to another care facility in the event of deterioration of health.

Disadvantages to this type of care

■ They tend to be larger establishments which may lack a homely feel.

■ Being one of a large number of consumers can be isolating.

■ Costs can be high.

Some questions you should ask yourself when considering a nursing home as an option

■ Can the individual cope with being one of a large number of consumers?

■ Will this environment be detrimental or stimulating to their mental well-being?

■ Can they cope with an environment which, because of its size, may have less flexible routines than residential care?

RESPITE AND REHABILITATION

Many residential and nursing homes offer respite or rehabilitation care. If your situation requires such a service, you will need to decide whether the care home setting is right or whether staying at home with support is a more viable option.

You may be aware that *respite* is sometimes required when there is a person caring for their loved one at home and this carer wishes to go away for a period of rest. Or the primary carer may themselves become ill or require hospitalisation thus leaving their charge in need of help. The consumer of this type of care is one in need of a temporary care solution. Consequently, a care home is often a viable short-term choice.

Millions of people aged 50 and over provide some sort of unpaid care to family or friends. So in theory, this means that there are potentially millions of people in need of some form of respite from their position as carer and these respite breaks will sometimes be funded by the local authority for up to six weeks per year. Consumers might return to the same care home on a regular basis for several weeks at a time and form good relationships with staff and other residents.

When finding a home offering respite facilities, questions should be asked with as much thoroughness as when care is being sought on a long-term basis. You should still put as much effort into planning respite care, because even two weeks can seem like a lifetime to the consumer if the wrong choice of home is made.

Questions when arranging rehabilitation care

If arranging *rehabilitation care*, ask the same questions you would ask a nursing home, with some additions such as:

■ Can long-term rehabilitation objectives can be realistically achieved within the care home setting?

■ Does the home have a high turnover of staff or poor sickness records?

■ Will the well-being of the consumer depend on one or two key members of staff? For example, you will need to feel confident that the home's physiotherapy or chosen rehabilitation process *can* and *will* be carried out by a number of key people working together, but who are *not entirely interdependent* on each other.

Some nursing home facilities are fantastic in terms of rehabilitation, and have the most magnificent features such as hydro pools. However, don't assume that high-tech facilities translate to quality care. When rehabilitating, individuals need a continuous amount of support, encouragement, praise, pushing and reassurance that things will get better (if they will) or honesty if progress is not being or likely to be made. These things are achieved by people – good, well-trained people – and are not purely down to environment.

When choosing a home for rehabilitation, if that home is not a purpose-built facility, ask questions that can be measured with real outcomes, such as how successful the home has been at rehabilitating others with the same condition. Only then will you be able to make an informed choice as to whether that home is right for your circumstances.

Whether the home you choose to view is purpose-built for respite or rehabilitation, or a nursing/residential facility, you should still establish the quality of the care provided.

REMEMBER

Don't make the mistake of thinking that you don't need to be as thorough because care is required only short term

---

7

Domiciliary Care

Domiciliary care is a fast-growing sector of the health and social care industry and the one with the most variables. Because of these variables, domiciliary care can appear to offer the most 'tailored' service or it can be difficult because the choices can appear confusing. So this chapter requires much more of an introduction than the previous one on care homes, but I do simplify the options. I cover the following:

- daily care services
- live-in care services
- employment agencies.

Respite and rehabilitation care is also mentioned within this section.

Both daily and live-in care services can be delivered either by way of a *service provider* or an *employment agency* and you need to know that there is a fundamental difference between the two. The point has been confused because the NMCS refer to all domiciliary care organisations as agencies and therefore many service providers will still refer to themselves by this term, even if they are a service provider.

SERVICE PROVIDER

A *service provider* should provide a full service. This will include the organisation directly employing and paying care workers and providing consumers with support and advice around the clock. An indication that an organisation is a service will include them having control over what the worker wears and how they conduct themselves, so uniforms are a fairly clear indication of a *service* rather than an *agency*. They will provide training and policies for their workers, pay wages and hire and fire them. Unfortunately some organisations will do all of these things but still claim to be an agent. Most of them do so *not* out of deceit *but* out of ignorance. The problem with ignorance is that an organisation may not have sufficient insurance cover if a problem arises, because they have bought an insurance policy for an agency rather than one for a service provider.

In my role as a management consultant I have witnessed care organisations that are clearly providing a service but are paying only national insurance contributions that have been deducted at source from the workers *but not* the employer contributions. Should this come to light – and it is likely to if the Inland Revenue undertakes a routine inspection – then a care organisation could be faced with owing large sums of money. If they do not have available funds they could potentially be put out of business. Ignorance of the law is no defence and you don't want to find that the chosen care organisation has been declared bankrupt! So even if the provider does not know their obligations in law, you should try to understand them. Some organisations expect consumers to pay fees in advance.

EMPLOYMENT AGENCY

It is not difficult to identify an employment agency as they will usually just introduce care workers, and consumer and worker will need to agree between themselves the terms of employment. Some agencies will offer guidance on the level of pay and conditions that a worker might be willing to accept, but agencies will not usually provide ongoing support or advice after the introduction. Such a withdrawal of support and advice after the introduction of a worker by an agency is normal practice, and the CSCI exclude employment agencies from certain obligations within the NMCS. You will see in Part 2 which obligations they are excluded from as it is clearly indicated.

HOW TO IDENTIFY WHICH IS WHICH

When talking to domiciliary organisations you should consider the following:

- Clarify if they are inspected against all care standards and if so confirm that they see themselves as a 'service provider' and not as an 'agent'. If they say that they *must* adhere to all of the care standards, that they *are* a service provider and they *do* pay employer's national insurance etc. then the organisation has a clear understanding of their status.

- If they say that they *are* inspected for all standards but that they *see* themselves as an agent then you must clarify this point. Do they simply mean that they 'call themselves an agent' or do they mean that they do not pay employer's national insurance? If it is the latter you should proceed with caution.

■ If it is clear that an organisation considers itself an agent then you must ask what it means to the consumer in terms of responsibility for workers etc.

■ If they claim to take all of the responsibility but have said that they do not pay employer's national insurance, then you must confirm that they hold full employers' liability insurance. If they do, then the risk you are taking by using such a service would appear to be an issue of future financial stability, if the Inland Revenue inspected and the organisation were deemed to be a service provider.

Quite what you might choose to do with any information you have is up to you. My aim is to protect the consumers of services and it is my knowledge of this sector and the ambiguity that has arisen over the years (due to the complexity of the debate over agent versus care provider) that encourages me to help you to educate yourself. It would be foolish of anyone (professional or layman) to assume that because an organisation provides services on behalf of a local authority that the position of agent/service provider is clear.

In the overview of the National Minimum Standards for Domiciliary Care Agencies, you will see that there are some standards from which agencies are totally excluded and others from which there is partial exemption. I have indicated exemption from the entire standard by stating this next to the standard number and title. For exclusion from part of the standard, I have indicated this next to the relevant paragraph, or have used an asterisk to indicate certain minor exclusions.

When formulating the care standards, policy-makers had to consider that domiciliary care services which elders buy into are sometimes the same services which many young disabled consumers buy into. This made the job of developing the standards difficult because what would suit a young consumer is different from that which would suit older people. The general feeling is that those buying into an employment agency arrangement do so because they want ultimate control over the care provided, and some, but not all, of the exemptions are such that there would be no way for an agency to have control over the worker. I believe this to be an accurate representation of why many young consumers of agency-provided care opt for this arrangement. However, I do not feel that this is the ultimate motivation for some older consumers and fear that the cost of care from a service provider versus an agency arrangement can be the greater motivating factor.

I quote a manager of one employment agency who, in my mind, has an excellent attitude to his relationship with the users of his service. Despite the fact that, in *theory*, the company doesn't have to provide after-sales support other than to provide replacement workers, he states that:

> *Any good employment agency should offer to solve any problems their clients report following introductions and this includes the suitability of workers. However, this does not and cannot extend to queries or complaints about a care worker's work/performance after the introduction has been made* unless *both care worker and client wish us to become involved (e.g. to attempt to resolve a disagreement), which we would be happy to do as a mediator on their mutual behalf.*

Do note the words 'any good employment agency' and look at the constraints that even a good one will face, in that intervention will be appropriate only if both parties agree to it. This is because there are legal limitations that agencies face in terms of what involvement they can have. There is no room here to examine the details, but I will mention that there are implications to this and employment law guidance sets out the relationship an agent should have with its consumers. The relevant authorities would need to be satisfied that, if a company claims to be an agent, they act in an agent-like fashion. If an employment agency offers *more* than is deemed to be appropriate for an agent, they could face being told that they have, in fact, become a service provider.

I give you this background so that you are clear on the limitations that some providers face, and that your expectations of what they can offer may be realistic. I also want to ensure that you are not left totally confused by the numerous differences between companies and their compliance obligations, because you may think that a company you are buying into will provide training for the care staff, but they are an agent and therefore will not.

Remember also that further confusion arises because the minimum standards for domiciliary care refer to *all providers* of domiciliary services as 'agencies' and differentiates the employment agencies only where necessary (as when excluding them from compliance) by describing them as those 'solely introducing workers'.

To lessen such confusion, I refer from here on (up to the end of Part 1) to those providing a care service as *service providers* and employment agencies are referred to as *agencies* – I wish the policy-makers had done the same!

In the remainder of this chapter I give a general overview of the different types of domiciliary care available and begin with service providers (daily care and live-in care services) and then move on to the role of agencies. I will discuss the pros and cons of each and encourage you to ask yourself questions about the feasibility of this care.

Unlike care homes, where you can see tangible proof of claims such as 'our bedrooms are beautifully decorated and all are en-suite', with domiciliary care there is little to judge until an individual is in receipt of the service. This makes my job of introducing this type of care longer, because I wish to be much more thorough.

In Chapter 10 on 'arranging domiciliary care services' I go to great lengths to cover the questions you can ask and the observations you can make to safeguard your interests when choosing such care services. I hope that my introduction to the complexity and diversity of domiciliary care will encourage you to do the same.

I suspect you will already be formulating your preferred type of care based on the topics we have covered so far, such as how professionals can support your choices, particularly in light of the issues we addressed in Chapter 4 on 'care choices'. I encourage you to keep an open mind.

DAILY CARE SERVICES (SERVICE PROVIDER)

Domiciliary *daily* care can be arranged for key times, and visits are often arranged to assist individuals with a certain tasks such as:

- personal care
- shopping

- meal preparation
- assistance with medication
- helping an individual attend an appointment such as a hospital appointment
- helping users of day services attend them
- walking doges which some workers may be happy to do
- helping with children which some workers may be allowed to do.

In fact, any task can be included within reason as long as it is within a care worker's capability, it is on their employer's agreed task list and it doesn't compromise health and safety or relevant law. The organisation must also be registered to provide the service; for example, some care organisations are registered to care for children with disabilities or to care for the able-bodied children of the consumer of the service. If your situation is such that a care worker is expected to babysit, for example, do clarify that the service is registered to allow them to do so. This is because workers will need to have been checked against the Protection of Children Act register (POCA) and have training in child protection procedures. If the organisation does not routinely check POCA and a service for children or babysitting is a likely requirement of the job, then you would be ill advised to take your enquiry further until you are satisfied that the provider is registered to care for children. In some cases the provider themselves will be unaware of the need to be registered to care for children in such an informal setting, such as babysitting. This might be because either it has not been requested before *or* a CSCI inspector has not picked up on the fact that it is a service being provided, and so it has not been discussed with the care organisation.

Common examples of daily care services

Each care provider will hold a view on the hours and scope of service offered by its workers, but I have listed the most common arrangements. A popular schedule of daily care is:

- A morning visit to assist individuals to get up and dressed plus preparation of breakfast.

- A second visit made in the evening to assist with bedtime routines.

- Some consumers may require a lunch visit, or for a couple of days per week they may have additional hours for household assistance such as cleaning.

- Individuals may be cared for by family members during the day and merely require assistance at night in order not to disturb the main unpaid carer. Such cover can be provided either by way of a *sleep-in service* or a *night duty service*.

Sleep-in service

A sleep-in service will usually commence between 8 p.m. and 9 p.m. and run through until 7 a.m. or 8 a.m., depending on company policy, but an eleven-hour shift is normal.

During an eleven-hour period, a prudent care organisation would expect the care worker to have at least seven hours' sleep, as the purpose of performing a sleep-in duty is not to work for the duration, but to act as a back-up in the event that help or assistance is required during the night.

It would not be unreasonable to request that a sleep-in worker help an individual get ready for bed or up again in the morning, unless there was an assessed risk preventing them from doing this on their own. In this case, a second person would probably need to be employed to undertake that task with them or the main carer would need to be around to help. Part of the appeal of a sleep-in service is the ability to incorporate such tasks into the arrangement. Each company will have its views on what other tasks could be asked of a sleep-in care worker.

Sleep-in workers would usually expect a bedroom to sleep in, or at the very least a camp bed in a part of the house they could use privately, save for them being called should their assistance be required. Each company will have their own policy in respect of the conditions of the workplace it expects for its staff. Many people use a bell or a baby monitor to attract the attention of the sleeping worker.

If a worker is regularly woken more than twice during the period that it is agreed he or she will sleep, the service provider may insist that arrangements are changed to that of *night-duty* service.

Night-duty service

The Working Time Regulations place an onus of responsibility on employers (worth noting if you decide to employ a worker) to:

■ Make sure that workers are physically and mentally fit enough to undertake night-duty work *and* that anyone undertaking the work is doing so willingly.

■ Offer a free health assessment to any worker who is to become a night worker and also provide the opportunity to have further assessments at regular intervals.

- Take all reasonable steps to ensure that the 'normal' hours of their night workers do not exceed an average of 8 hours for each 24 hours over a 17-week period (extendable as for the 48-hour period above). The 'normal hours' are those fixed by the contract of employment and do not include overtime or leave.

- Keep adequate records to demonstrate, if required by the Health and Safety Executive, that the limits on night work are being observed. Records also need to be kept of health assessments.

- If a registered medical practitioner indicates that a worker is suffering from health problems connected to the fact that he/she works nights, he/she is entitled to be transferred, wherever possible, to other suitable work which is not at night.

This list is not exhaustive and there are of course other considerations that employers need to make in relation to the regulations.

Night-duty will be less cost-effective than a sleep-in service and in some cases can cost more than a 24-hour period of live-in care. This is because night-duty is charged by the hour and night staff can demand a premium. The rate of charge can for this reason often be more per hour than that charged during daylight hours.

Night care is sometimes provided for people who are very ill or physically vulnerable or those who require one or two hourly turns throughout the night. Alternatively, night care will suit the consumer who does not wish to go to bed until the early hours.

It would not be unusual to ask that a night-duty worker undertake some tasks aside from personal care. For example, many consumers of night care will request that some ironing be done. Views will differ between care providers and the hours of a night-duty worker will usually be similar to those of a sleep-in service. However, if you are paying for a night-duty worker, it is not unreasonable to expect them to be awake all night. This is, after all, exactly what you are paying for!

Terms and conditions

Over the years, in a bid to save money, Social Services have requested that domiciliary care providers be responsive and provide short visits to local authority-funded users of the service. As a result, providers are delivering care in as little as 15-minute blocks but it is questionable what can realistically be achieved in that time. Some organisations will reserve the right not to offer short visits to private, paying consumers while others may be willing to do so only if they have other users of their services within the immediate area. Such restrictions may be imposed for economic reasons.

The most standard terms of domiciliary care hours are that, whatever care you purchase, you purchase it in at least one-hour blocks. Most domiciliary care companies will offer *all* of their services on a respite basis.

Some companies will charge you travel expenses on top of the hourly rate of charge and others will have all-inclusive fees.

Many companies will apply an increased premium for evenings, weekends and public holidays.

Health and safety issues

As providers of domiciliary care services employ their workers, they have a duty of care towards them in respect of health and safety matters.

Therefore, as a minimum, workers should be supplied with gloves and, in some cases, aprons when undertaking care tasks of a personal nature. Such use of protective clothing is as much to protect those being cared for from any germs a care worker may be carrying as it is to protect the worker.

Consumers of a care service should not be expected to provide or to pay for personal protective clothing (PPC). If a care organisation tries to charge or insists that an individual buy these, I would suggest that, not only should the position be challenged, but the matter be referred to the CSCI.

Note
- If a consumer employs a worker (privately or via an agency), they will be responsible for providing PPC.
- If the worker is self-employed, then an agreement as to who should provide PPC must be reached between the consumer and the care worker.

More on health and safety

- In the event that it is identified that equipment is required to ensure the safety of the consumer and the worker when carrying out moving and handling tasks, then service providers could either provide equipment in the short term or assist individuals in obtaining it.

- Regardless of who has identified the need, service providers employ the care workers and they have a legal obligation to protect their workers. But organisations adopt different approaches to the need for equipment and some take such matters more seriously than others.

- If a need is identified that a consumer required a hoist, some companies might allow their care workers to continue handling until the hoist was made available. Others would insist that the consumer stayed in bed in the interim and disallow all handling until the hoist arrived, while some might adopt any range of approaches in between.

Whatever approach is taken, if an individual is told that they require some form of equipment by anyone other than the care provider, then the care provider must be informed so that they can consider the safety issues pending delivery of equipment. Don't assume that whoever assessed the need (even if it is Social Services) will automatically let the care provider know. Not knowing may mean a care provider will not be able to give their care workers the protection they deserve – through no fault of their own.

What about domestic chores?

You will also notice that, at the beginning of this chapter, I listed some tasks which could be reasonably expected of a care worker, and cleaning was not one of them. This is because service providers hold different views on whether they will allow care staff to undertake light household duties or not. Therefore, should regular assistance with household cleaning be required, clarify this at the initial stages of arranging care with a daily care provider. If an organisation appears apprehensive about allowing care workers to undertake domestic duties, it could be due to staff shortages or health and safety concerns.

> **REMEMBER**
> Service providers employ their workers and employment laws mean that they have obligations towards them.

Those who will allow domestic chores to be undertaken usually allow only the most basic and light of household duties, for example restricted to vacuuming *around* heavy objects and polishing.

If care is funded by the local authority, then clarify with the social worker which duties can be requested from a care provider. Some authorities will not fund services if the need consists purely/mostly of cleaning. If they discover that care staff are being utilised in this way, they may reduce or in some cases even remove services depending on other duties the worker may be performing.

Who will daily care suit?

Domiciliary daily care may suit several types of people including:

- Those with a partner or family member willing to assist with other aspects of daily living between domiciliary care worker visits.

- Those who are able, once up and out of bed, to undertake basic daily tasks such as making a drink.

- Those who are out during the day either at day services, workplaces or similar.

- Those whose physical or medical condition does *not* render them at risk by being left alone.

This type of service may not suit individuals if:

- They are unable to call for help between care worker visits.

- They are at risk of falling or could suffer the ill effects of a condition such as choking if left for long periods of time.

- They have a very changeable condition.

- They are unable to undertake basic daily tasks such as making a drink.

Advantages of this type of care

- It enables individuals to remain in their own home.

- It enables them to be in control of their own time schedule (to a point).

- The provision of it is not determined by illness (to a point) in that an individual, for example, may have a severe disability, but if they have someone such as a partner who can help with basic tasks throughout the day, then domiciliary care workers can assist them with the fundamental personal care tasks at key times.

- It can be delivered in conjunction with other support services such as those of district nursing provision.

- It often affords more privacy and autonomy than a residential environment can realistically offer.

Domiciliary daily care can be cost-effective for up to eight hours per day but if more hours are required, then live-in care at home should be considered, because the price for 24-hour live-in care becomes comparable with daily care exceeding eight hours.

Disadvantages of daily care

- Problems can arise due to a service provider's time and staffing constraints. For example, if the agency has 40 consumers requiring assistance at 7 a.m. and only 20 care staff, then 50 per cent of the users of the service will have to compromise their schedule.

- Evening routines can be limited because many service providers will not allow care staff to work beyond 10 p.m. This means if an hour is required to get ready for bed, workers will have to start at 9 p.m. If consumers prefer a much later bedtime, then daily care may not be able to offer the flexibility required.

- Users of domiciliary daily care can be vulnerable to missed visits. This is not unheard of either when a care worker is ill but doesn't call their office in time for managers to notify consumers, or the visit has just been overlooked. It is worth asking any daily agency what their incidence rate of forgotten visits is.

- Certain areas may have a shortage of care workers or problems with retention of workers due to fierce competition with other providers or agencies. This can lead to a large turnover of staff which in turn may mean a large volume of care workers, thus causing continuity problems.

- Where care providers do have reliable staff and they provide good levels of continuity, there is a danger of individuals becoming too dependent on a small number of workers, which can make change (if necessary at any time) much harder to cope with.

■ Unless a care provider can give a cast iron guarantee that care workers are going to be reliable, I would not recommend this type of care for anyone choosing to stay at home during a period of intensive rehabilitation, especially one that relies on care workers arriving on time to accompany a consumer to appointments such as physiotherapy. If the administration teams responsible for scheduling care workers' visits, are unfamiliar with a certain area and associated problems such as traffic hotspots, they can have a tendency not to allow enough time between care worker visits. If a consumer is second in a group of three morning calls it would not be uncommon for the second call to be shortened in a bid for the care worker to make up for lost time. The care standards do address this issue and the CSCI would not approve of such shortening of visits on a regular basis, but it does happen. If it happens occasionally, due to a crash on a notorious road or bad weather, then this would be out of the control of the service provider and care worker. But it is a point you should consider carefully when choosing this type of service and be sure you enquire about the travel time allocated between visits.

LIVE-IN CARE SERVICE (SERVICE PROVIDER)

Live-in care can be a great alternative to residential or nursing home services, but it is not a practical alternative for everyone.

If care needs are such that they can be dealt with by one person, then staying at home with live-in assistance can, in some cases, be just as cost-effective as a nursing home. Social Services are starting to buy into live-in care on a more regular basis.

Where a couple both require care, as can often be the case with older people, such an arrangement can be especially advantageous financially. Couples can stay together, something which cannot always be guaranteed if nursing home accommodation is sought.

Most live-in care provision is provided on a continuous and ongoing basis but there are those who merely use a live-in service for respite needs, or in blocks of allocated time to aid rehabilitation or to provide back-up for a privately-employed care worker.

The minimum amount of time that a live-in care provider would usually deliver care is a continuous period of 48 hours and then any number of additional hours beyond that. For example, you could have 69 hours of care starting on Friday at 12 noon and finishing on Monday at 9 a.m.

Typical tasks provided by live-in care workers

As with daily care, live-in care workers provided via a service provider would normally be able to undertake tasks such as:

- all aspects of personal care

- shopping

- meal preparation

- assistance with medication

- helping an individual attend an appointment such as a hospital

- helping users of day services attend them or alternatively arranging social activities both inside or outside the home

- care for pets

- helping with the general running of the household such as facilitating the paying of bills

- driving (where necessary)

- being available at night in the event of an emergency.

Sleep-in and night-duty services

I mentioned in the section above on domiciliary daily care that some daily care companies offer sleep-in and night-duty services. I also identified that continuity of staffing can be a problem. An alternative is that some live-in care providers are willing to provide care workers who undertake sleep-in duties and night duties. This can be provided as long as you can demonstrate to them that the care worker will not be taken advantage of and made to work day and night. In the event that they have worked at night, you must ensure that they will *realistically* be able to catch up on their sleep during the day. It would therefore be worth talking to a provider if this is your requirement.

Advantages of using a live-in care worker for provision of care

- They are already on site, so late arrival and no-shows are avoided.

- A better level of continuity is provided.

- It can be as cost-effective as daily care (depending on the number of daily hours required – but in the case of night-duty, probably more so).

■ There is more scope for flexibility. For example, if an individual is out late one night, the worker would be on-site already and should be able to respond to a change of schedule.

Living arrangements

Live-in care workers would require, as an absolute minimum, a bedroom with a wardrobe. Some companies insist on workers having their own bathroom. I think this is a clear indication of the type of clientèle such companies wish to attract. Whatever one's social standing or home environment, consumers of care should be apprehensive of buying into a service with a single-minded attitude regarding any aspect of that service. Everyone has a right to quality care, and anyone claiming to provide care should be looking beyond merely the ability to provide a care worker with their own bathroom. I do not believe such an attitude to be the right spirit for this type of service provision. The attraction of live-in care is its adaptability to meet the needs of the majority of individuals. The person requiring care is who should matter most, and care workers should assist an individual to live each day as they wish.

Night support

With care delivered by a service provider, there should be an agreed plan of care (plans of care are covered at greater length in Part 2) which would normally have a specified cut-off point at which a care worker would effectively no longer be on duty. Live-in workers should be available in the event of an emergency during the night. But if they are regularly being woken during the period that it is agreed they will sleep, the service provider may insist (and any responsible company would insist) that the arrangement is changed and a second care worker brought in to provide night care, because no care worker who is living-in on a full-time basis could possibly provide a safe level of care if they are deprived of sleep.

The level of night support a live-in care worker can offer will be dependent upon the organisation's own philosophy. There are service providers who will allow care workers to be disturbed regularly at night and continue to work the next day with no way of catching up on lost sleep as long as the consumer pays an additional fee each time they disturb the worker.

I can see no advantages with such an arrangement, only the potential for abuse by either party. For example, if an individual has dementia and there is nobody else within the household *who can verify the number of wake up calls?* Although the individual is vulnerable to financial abuse, *what about the care worker?* If they are continually being woken at night but their employer feels that money is sufficient compensation for sleep deprivation, at what point does the worker say enough is enough?

Worryingly there is the health and safety aspect of such an arrangement because an extra £20 a night in their pay packet won't make a care worker any less tired. If a care worker is tired, they won't be alert nor will they be very patient – *and* do not forget that employers also have obligations in law in respect of work undertaken at night.

Travelling expenses

Almost all live-in care companies will charge for a care worker's travelling expenses on top of the 24-hourly rate of charge and most will charge an increased premium for public holidays, usually at least double.

Associated costs

There will also be the associated costs of having a care worker living in a consumer's home and, at the very least, workers will need to be provided with three meals a day. It would be rare to expect consumers to provide care workers with toiletries or luxury items, but if they have special dietary requirements these should be accommodated.

Well-organised care providers will ensure arrangements are clarified and provide written details for the consumer in respect of the associated costs of a care worker. This should include the conditions stipulating when to pay for additional things for care workers – such as cinema entry fees. This is discussed in Chapter 10 on arranging domiciliary care services in a little more detail

Health and safety issues

As previously mentioned, providers of domiciliary care services employ their workers and have a duty of care towards them in respect of health and safety matters. To recap – and those who have read the section on daily care services above will see the repetition here – as a minimum, workers should be supplied with gloves and, in some cases, aprons when undertaking care tasks of a personal nature. Such use of protective clothing is as much to protect those being cared for from any germs a care worker may be carrying as it is to protect the worker.

Consumers of a care service should not be expected to provide or to pay for personal protective clothing (PPC). If a care organisation tries to charge or insists that an individual buy these, I would suggest that, not only should the position be challenged, but the matter be referred to CSCI.

> **Note**
> - If a consumer employs a worker (privately or via an agency), they will be responsible for providing PPC.
> - If the worker is self-employed, then an agreement as to who should provide PPC must be reached between the consumer and the care worker.

Safety equipment

Still on the matter of health and safety, in the event that it is identified that equipment is required to ensure the safety of the consumer and the worker when carrying out moving and handling tasks, then service providers could either provide equipment in the short-term or assist individuals in obtaining it. Regardless of who has identified the need, service providers employ the care workers and they have a legal obligation to protect them. But organisations adopt different approaches to the need for equipment and some take such matters more seriously than others.

If a need is identified that a consumer requires a hoist, some companies would allow their care workers to continue handling until the hoist was made available. Others would insist that the consumer stayed in bed in the interim and disallow all handling until the hoist arrived, while some might adopt any range of approaches in between.

Whatever approach is taken, if a consumer is told that some form of equipment is required and the advice comes from anyone other than the care provider, the provider must be notified. This is so that they are given an opportunity to discuss the options with individuals during the time between assessment and the delivery of equipment. Don't assume that whoever assessed the need (even if it is Social Services) will automatically let the care provider know. If the provider is unaware of changing mobility problems they will not be able to protect their care workers. A live-in care worker must also assume responsibility for letting his or her employer know about any changes in health or environment.

What about domestic chores?

At the beginning of this chapter I listed some tasks which could reasonably be expected of a care worker, and cleaning was not one of them. Service providers hold different views on whether they will allow workers to undertake light household duties. Should regular assistance with household cleaning be required, clarify this at the initial stages of dealing with a care provider. If a company appears apprehensive about allowing care workers to undertake domestic duties, it could be linked with health and safety concerns as previously mentioned. Remember – service providers employ their workers and therefore have legal obligations to fulfil. Those who will allow domestic chores to be carried out will usually allow only the most basic and light of household duties even if the care worker is living-in.

Some live-in care workers may enjoy gardening and offer to undertake tasks such as mowing the lawn, but do speak with the care provider before allowing workers to do anything you are not absolutely sure is permitted. Care workers, if adequately trained, should be fully conversant with the dos and don'ts of their employment.

Break times

Most care providers will expect their staff to have a minimum break of at least two hours daily (continuous) so they would no doubt ask whether the consumer can be left alone for any periods of time throughout the day. If they can't then discussion must be had with the provider regarding alternative arrangements to be made to give a worker rest breaks. Some companies will allow breaks to be taken on the premises, but there are many variables and options you might be offered, depending on the provider. Rest breaks are also addressed under the Working Time Regulations, thus placing an onus of responsibility on the employer to balance the needs of workers and consumers.

Who are the care workers?

Another consideration to be made is whether a consumer would be willing to have a younger person caring for them because live-in work attracts younger workers. Not all live-in care companies provide such a workforce, but it is fair to say that young overseas workers from Australia, New Zealand, South Africa, Zimbabwe and much of Eastern and Central Europe make up the workforce that dominates this sector of care services. Some workers are free to work in the UK without restriction while others are on working holiday visas, the rules regarding which frequently change. As at February 2006, holders of a visa are allowed to work for only one year of the two-year visa duration. Technically if working beyond this period, a care worker would be doing so illegally.

When live-in care is delivered by a service provider, it is unlikely that a consumer would be able to meet a worker in advance of them arriving to provide the care. This is because logistically it would be difficult for most companies to arrange. It is also fair to say that consumers are paying the organisation to provide a full service, part of which is the provider knowing the individual's needs. It is important that there is a trust that the provider will find a suitable care giver without consumers having to meet the worker first. Reassurance should be offered that in the event an individual does not like a worker, they are replaced.

Length of stay

Some live-in workers may stay for two weeks, meaning that consumers have a new person with that regularity. Others may stay for a minimum of three months and others may offer any range of periods between the two. If the duration of a care worker's stay is determined by a well-run care organisation they will always endeavour to offer continuity and will know that the most successful approach will be to allow workers and consumers to decide between themselves when it would be suitable for the worker to have time off. If a care worker wanted to travel every four or five weeks, they could stay with the same consumer for four to five weeks at a time and then take a week or weekend off to travel, returning when their trip ends for another agreed period. Such an arrangement will mean individuals have the continuity of a full-time worker. When they are replaced, it becomes less relevant whether the replacement is liked or not because it would be for only a short time until the main worker returns. It would be unusual for an organisation to provide the same regular care worker to replace a permanent worker, so even where organisations offer long-term workers, individuals should be prepared for new faces during time-off periods.

Involvement of the service provider

A service provider should assume responsibility for the running of a care package as this is what they are paid to do, but the level at which they will be involved is something individuals will need to establish at the enquiry stages.

Good care providers will be involved (with the consumer's agreement) with an individual's family, district nurses or other associated professionals. They will provide regular support and supervision both of consumers and workers. Others will do only what is required of them to adhere to the care standards. The variation between companies can be vast. Some providers give a seamless care service with their employees working seven days per week. Others insist that workers be given one day per week free and consumers must make their own arrangements.

Combinations of service provision

Individual circumstances will dictate which services are bought into, but it is possible to combine live-in support with daily assistance. So if someone really likes a care organisation but they offer only a six-day per week service, don't eliminate them but instead utilise a second company to bridge the gap. Alternatively, employ an individual privately for one day per week.

Some organisations will let care staff cook for a consumer's family if they visit, others won't. While some will allow workers to go on holiday with consumers or drive their car, others will not. The variables are endless so I stop here and hope that any other questions about live-in care will be answered by the companies as you approach them – should this be the type of care chosen.

Summary

To wrap this section up, let's look at the pros and cons in brief.

Advantages of this type of care

■ Care is one-on-one.

■ If a couple both require care, it may be more cost-effective than both going into a care home and their relationship remains unaltered.

■ Care is delivered in a familiar environment.

■ Individuals are living by their own house rules.

■ Individuals are empowered to continue to make meaningful decisions such as what the care worker is to buy for dinner and how the home is run.

■ Individuals continue to live within a community in which they are already established.

■ If a good care provider is chosen, there will be continuity of care staff and an opportunity to develop long-standing relationships with the care workers while being mindful of the professional boundaries.

■ There will be flexibility of living by one's own timetable, within reason.

■ If supervised regularly, care should be of sound quality as it is delivered in a very tailored way.

Disadvantages of this type of care

■ There is still an associated cost of running the home on top of the expense of care.

■ Care workers' living expenses need to be met, so pound for pound it can be a more expensive option than a nursing home if just one person is receiving care.

■ Individuals can become too attached to care staff who stay long term.

- Frequent changes of care worker can make individuals unsettled.

- An ability to trust care staff almost immediately is essential.

- Although live-in care is available UK-wide, the majority of the services are based in the south of England and can therefore be expensive.

- If there are other household members, they may find the presence of a care worker intrusive at times.

EMPLOYMENT AGENCIES

You will see in Chapter 8 on privately employing care staff that I am a little apprehensive about directly employing care workers due to the enormity of the task, and a good compromise is to use an employment agency. Employing workers via an agency and paying the organisation a weekly fee usually ensures that they will deal with issues such as recruitment on behalf of the consumer.

If a consumer suffers from any condition that leaves them particularly vulnerable, such as dementia, or where there is no immediate family member to overview the situation, then I would discourage any form of private employment, even via an agency. An agency cannot be responsible for workers once a consumer has employed them. If a person does not have the capacity to report concerns about their treatment by a worker (as may be the case with a person suffering dementia) then they are at a disadvantage. When care is supplied by a service provider, regular visits and monitoring of the situation should afford greater protection because the supervisors should be able to pick up on any changes in the behaviour of the consumer that may be linked to poor treatment. This is not true of an agency arrangement as there would not be any supervisory visits. However, an agency arrangement works very well for a lot of people.

As you will be aware from my introduction to the chapter on domiciliary care, the NMCS governs areas concerning the running of domiciliary care, but not all care standards apply to employment agencies. Within the overview of the standards, I have made it clear which ones do *not* apply.

If using an agency:

- Consumers will not need to advertise for workers, which can be costly.

- Workers will have been screened to ensure that they do not have a criminal record, something which, if employing privately without the help of an agency, consumers will not be at liberty to do.

Interviewing candidates

Using an employment agency will often involve consumers, or someone on their behalf, interviewing each of the candidates. It should be clarified at the outset whether an employment agency will expect consumers to do so.

If consumers are expected to interview workers, read Chapter 8 on private employment to gain some valuable insights and useful techniques.

Employment agencies will differ in their approach and, while some may provide guidance on the terms and conditions which should be offered to workers, others may not.

Level of service provision

Because an employment agency merely introduces workers, there is nothing in the way of service provision to discuss. This does not mean that the agency will not be available to help you to find another worker should the chosen candidate not be suitable, but it is essential to understand that as a rule they only introduce workers. If an agency is offering a greater level of involvement, then realistically they *could be seen to be offering a service.* If this were the case, then there is an argument that the company should be adhering to *all* of the minimum care standards. Again I would urge you to clarify the position of the organisation for the protection of the person requiring care.

Care workers introduced should be able to offer either daily care or live-in services, but this does depend on what the individual employment agency offers.

Advantages of this type of care

- Can be cheaper than employing a service provider.

- Consumers are likely to meet the care worker first.

- Consumers will not need to advertise.

- Care workers should already have criminal record clearance and references should have been taken, making it safe to interview them within the consumer's home.

- Good agencies will provide all the information needed in respect of the engagement of a worker, including the consumer's obligations in law.

Disadvantages of this type of care

■ Time-consuming if interviewing many candidates, which may happen if a situation is a complex one.

■ If the interviewer lacks technique care workers may be scared off.

■ If the choice of agency is one that does not give advice in respect of employment issues, then consumers will themselves need to look into the legality of arranging to pay employer's national insurance contributions *or* be sure that the worker is self-employed.

■ Consumers will need to be sure they have adequate insurance cover in the event that a care worker was injured at work etc.

■ There is usually no back-up if there is a problem, but agencies will find a replacement worker if requested to do so.

8

Private Employment

HOW TO APPROACH PRIVATE EMPLOYMENT

Private employment will require a completely different approach to buying care from a service provider or an employment agency (although the section on employment agencies in the previous chapter can be used in conjunction with this one). Private employment of a care worker within one's home has no government-imposed standards against which it may be assessed. I feel that in many ways this puts those who privately employ in a particularly vulnerable position and for this reason I have included practical tips and helpful guidance on aspects of private employment in a bid to better safeguard those who choose this care choice. This advice will help even if you are using an employment agency.

What I cannot enter into is the legal position of employing at home. This includes issues such as:

- If the consumer is the employer, what specific responsibilities does this impose upon them?

- If the care worker is self-employed, what might that mean for the consumer?

For advice on such matters alternative guidance should be sought.

I also include this chapter on private employment to ensure that consumers can make informed choices and in a bid to offer as much help as I can to protect consumer interests.

A personal view of private employment

I personally do not see private employment as an advantageous care choice. I started my career as a care worker in 1984 and never once did it cross my mind to work privately for an individual. On reflection, I am pleased that I never considered it as an option because I can't see *any* advantages to working privately. However, I can see the following disadvantages:

- In the event of a problem, I would have no senior colleague to turn to for advice.

- If I had been unable to care for the consumer because of my own sickness or personal plans such as holidays, who would have provided the care?

- If a relationship had soured, the consumer would be left without care and I would have to start my career all over again.

- I would never have been exposed to the wealth of knowledge other co-workers have imparted to me over the years.

- I can see that as a teenager (which I was when my career started) I may have been tempted not to pay national insurance and income tax if I had the option of being paid cash in hand.

WHAT TYPE OF PERSON WORKS PRIVATELY?

Given that my job is to heighten consumer awareness and to safeguard their interests, my focus has to be on alerting you to the fact that *some people* who choose this route to becoming a care worker may do so for one or a combination of the following reasons:

■ They want to do things their way and so prefer independence from an employer.

■ They are hiding something.

■ They cannot provide a plausible work history.

■ They have tried to become employed but have failed.

■ They are working illegally and realise that many people privately employing will not undertake rigorous checks into their background.

■ They have a criminal record. (If you are able to find a worker who has already undergone a criminal records bureau check, then this will be an advantage, because otherwise you are not in a position to undertake a check yourself.)

■ They want to avoid paying income tax and national insurance.

Advantage of this type of care

With the above in mind, I would say that the advantage (in the singular) of this type of care is:

■ It is possible that it may be cheaper.

Disadvantages of this type of care

■ To have someone in a private household who is not answerable to a higher authority, such as an employer, suggests that all the responsibility for that person falls onto the consumer.

■ A robust back-up plan will be needed if the worker is sick or requires a holiday.

■ Care workers may be set on living by their own rules with no recourse for the consumer.

■ Without access to thorough vetting methods, consumers might employ a worker who has a problematic past.

■ Consumers are vulnerable to workers faking their experience. A common trick is that a friend will pretend to be a referee and say that the person has worked for them. In reality, they have no plausible work history or do not have one which they want to reveal.

■ Unless the interviewer is aware of how documents should look (such as work permits) they could potentially (regardless of whether intentionally) be breaking the law by employing an illegal worker.

■ A worker could have a criminal record or be listed on the protection of vulnerable adults list (POVA) or child protection register (POCA) as unsuitable to work with that category of people – but as private individuals, consumers are unable to freely access this information.

Background checks you can make

Consumers can contact their area CSCI department to enquire about local organisations running 'umbrella body schemes'. These are organisations registered to undertake Criminal Record Bureau checks (CRB), including the POCA and POVA checks, and will do so on behalf of a third-party care organisation. Consumers should endeavour to reach an agreement with an umbrella body to run checks on their behalf. Such an association, if they were in agreement (and there is no obligation by law for them to do so) will no doubt come at a cost but if such an arrangement is within one's means, then it will definitely be money well spent.

If you are still sure that employing privately is the ideal care choice, what should you do now?

What the consumer and worker agree to in terms of hours required and remuneration is entirely up to them, but first someone needs to be employed.

Below I share with you my experiences. These are not reflective of any specific school of thought in terms of recruitment processes, merely my tried and tested methods over many years in a professional capacity. I want to help to make recruiting as easy and safe as possible.

ADVERTISING

As mentioned in Chapter 1 on finding services, *The Lady* magazine runs linage adverts and often individuals advertise as workers looking for care work. I warned against recruiting in this way because publications cannot vet individuals advertising their services in this manner.

A compromise is that consumers place an advertisement in *The Lady* looking for a care worker and either:

- provide a PO box number for replies *or*

- buy a pay-as-you-go mobile telephone which can be used for the sole purpose of recruitment *or*

- set up an e-mail account for the same. This way the consumer is retaining the overall control of the recruitment process while not providing personal details in a public manner.

Mobile phone or e-mail is preferable to maximise responses because many people working in the care sector will not bother to write for a job as accessing work is so easy via telephone and e-mail.

Other suggestions for advertising
- in a publication of your choice

- on www.thegumtree.com – an online resource for overseas workers living in the UK and looking for work

- *TNT* – a free magazine aimed at the same workforce as the Gum Tree.

What do you include in the advert?
When writing an advert, it is advisable to give a clear indication of:

- the salary and benefits being offered
- the location
- whether experience is required

- if a driver is required and whether a car is provided *or* if applicants must be owner/drivers
- the hours of work
- whether accommodation is included
- a basic description of the person to be cared for.

As linage ads are charged by the word, you want maximum impact in the minimum amount of words while ensuring that applicants are aware of what is required of them. For example, you should specify if you require a driver otherwise everyone's time is wasted if non-drivers apply.

Here is an example of an advert that covers all of the basics:

> Experienced female care worker 25+ required to live with 85-year-old man with limited mobility in Hampstead Heath area – 5 days per week (£70.00 daily) for a minimum of one year. Must be car driver and like animals. Interested?
> Contact Mr Green on 00772 345678.

This is a count of 44 words and the advert covers everything an applicant would need initially to know.

DEALING WITH RESPONSES

Once responses to an advert start to roll in (but please don't be too disappointed if they don't, because recruitment is a difficult process) you need to be ready with a list of questions for candidates. You must also be observant as to the types of questions they are asking you. The following information will assist you if an applicant is taken through to the interview stage.

Questions to ask applicants

Questions to ask applicants should include (but are not limited to) the following. You should briefly write their responses down:

■ What work they have been doing for the last three years.

■ Whether they can verify their work history. You can agree to accept a copy of a reference that is already written, but make it clear that you will still need to speak with past employers directly. Do not accept mobile phone numbers for a work history where you are told it was with a company or a nursing home.

■ Whether they require a work permit and, if so, whether they have one.

■ If employed, the length of time they can commit to.

■ Whether they have a Criminal Record Bureau check (CRB) and, if so, can they bring the certificate to the interview? If they do not have one, ask them if they would be willing to allow you to undertake a check on their behalf. Even if you have no means of accessing a criminal record check, always ask this question because, if they don't have anything to hide, they will agree; if they do have something to hide, they might be forced to be honest if they think that you might find out about it anyway. It is worth noting that not all criminal records would stop me from employing a person. While you have a right to know about any convictions (even those deemed spent) do not allow yourself to be prejudiced against any applicant who is honest about a less-than-perfect past if the conviction disclosed is one that is unlikely to be relevant now; for example a 30-year-old applicant who has had an adult lifetime of good character but at 12 was arrested for shoplifting. In some ways such openness should be seen as a positive for the candidate.

■ Whether they have photographic identification and, if so, whether they can produce it.

■ Why they are looking to work privately as opposed to working for a company or through an agency.

Responses which should concern you

The following comments should concern you or require further questioning:

■ 'I haven't been working for the last three years.' If this is the case, question further to find out whether they have been on benefits, studying, etc. If no plausible explanation is given, end the conversation.

■ 'I can't verify my work history because the lady I was caring for has died' (or the home closed down or any combination of reasons may be given). My advice would be as above. Unless you can gain concrete proof of what someone has been doing, you are leaving yourself open to problems. In the case of someone saying that a care home has closed down, you could speak with the CSCI to clarify this point.

■ 'I don't need a work permit because I have this letter from the Home Office/I am married to a Brit/I have a permit but my passport is with immigration etc.' Ensure you verify any documentation you are given if you bring forward for interview anyone who is clearly non-EU and would ordinarily require a work permit. (I provide guidance later in the chapter.)

■ 'I can stay for [whatever the period of time is that you have specified within your advert].' If someone is confirming a period of stay, you must write this into an agreement of employment and ensure that this allows you to recover the cost of additional recruitment expenses if the person leaves before the agreed period. You will need to agree a trial period during which either party must be free to part ways without any costs being incurred.

■ If someone states that they have a Criminal Record Bureau Certificate but claim never to have worked for a care provider, then you must question how they came to possess the certificate as care workers cannot apply directly. If obtained via another employer outside of care, it may be that the check is a standard one and not an enhanced disclosure, which means the POVA list will not have been checked.

■ 'I want to work privately because I have my own company/I don't want to pay taxes/I don't want a company telling me what to do.' All of these responses could have certain implications and you should therefore make sure you question further.

Responses by phone

Applicants may want to discuss key points on the phone with you prior to agreeing to meet, and you should be willing to give basic details. However, don't give away too much as you want an opportunity to meet the person first and you don't want to risk scaring them off if a situation sounds more complicated in theory than it is in reality.

Give some basic points but if they ask too many questions (not a bad thing but you must retain control of the situation), explain that you will bring along a full job description and terms of employment which they will have every chance to read before the interview. This will give a professional vibe which will impress the potentially serious candidates and will scare off timewasters or any that may have thought that they were going to worm their way into a naïve individual's home.

INTERVIEWING

Another safety measure I wish to encourage is to initially interview applicants away from the home and in a public place, such as a hotel café (something which most hotels have and which are often very comfortable) or similar. Take someone along as not only is there is safety in numbers, but it will be valuable to have a second opinion. Where necessary, gain the permission of the venue.

If you are reading this section because you need to interview workers from an employment agency, they should have already been vetted and had police clearance, so in theory it should be fine to see them at home. But do check with the agency that they are in receipt of criminal record checks before agreeing to interview candidates.

Application forms

You should always ensure that candidates complete an application form for many reasons and they should do so in your presence (although you should give them a little space and privacy to do so). I suggest this for the following reasons:

■ To ensure that the person completes the form themselves.

■ To monitor the speed at which someone can answer such basic questions.

■ To cross-refer what you were told on the telephone (and you wrote in brief) against what is then written down on the application form. In the event that they lied their way into an interview, you are more likely to catch them out this way.

■ To refer back to at a later stage if there are any issues that arise once you have employed a care worker and they failed to disclose something of relevance.

You can devise a very basic application form on a personal computer and print it out or copy the layout of the one that follows later in the chapter.

Other documents

You should also provide:

■ a brief written description of the duties required of a worker
■ the benefits on offer
■ the hours of work
■ the conditions of employment

and give these to the applicant with the application form. This will save any wasted time in the event that the worker sees from the terms that there is something to which they cannot agree. This is far better than employing someone who is unhappy with a condition that they discover only once they accept the position. I have known private workers who didn't even unpack but instead turned around and walked straight out after discovering something they didn't like.

Conducting the interview

Once the application form is completed, the best way to conduct the interview is to talk through the form as this will raise all of the questions to which you require answers. For example, you could look at the applicant's nationality and then chat about their home country. As you go further down the form, talk about the experience they claim to have – where did they gain it etc.

Move through the form, chatting about any hobbies they may have disclosed and their cooking/housekeeping skills. Before you know it, you will have lots of relevant information pertaining to the person.

Tips and points worth bearing in mind when interviewing potential candidates

- You are not interviewing a replacement for the job of chief executive of a bank and, while I want to safeguard consumer interests, I also know what scares applicants off. You don't want to terrify the possibly genuine applicants you may attract, so be relaxed and interested in them as people and don't focus too much on academic experience. You will find that, with such a relaxed approach, you will learn more about the applicant than by stuffy, formal measures.

- Don't be too hung up on the way that an individual is dressed, especially if you are recruiting for a live-in position, as you want them to roll their sleeves up and muck in with the shopping, cleaning, etc. This doesn't mean that if someone is well turned out they should not be complimented for it, but if someone isn't so well-presented, don't make a big issue of it. Remember, it's what is on the inside that matters when looking for a care worker. However, if someone has body odour or appears unwashed, you should be concerned.

▪ You should remain in control of the interview but at the same time you must ensure that you give the applicant adequate time to respond to your questions.

▪ Try not to put a table between you and them.

▪ Give applicants an opportunity to ask you questions about the position.

▪ Always answer honestly, but focus on the positives. For example, if they ask whether they have their own bedroom and bathroom but they do not have the latter, then tell them this. Don't apologise for the fact that there is only one bathroom, but instead assure them that they will have privacy and that a routine will be worked out to accommodate them.

▪ Try to keep a friendly but professional attitude. Do not ask personal questions that could offend and that do not have a bearing on the position being offered, such as 'Are you gay?' or 'Do you have a boyfriend/girlfriend?'. You may hold views about such issues, but an interview is no place to discuss them. I accept that if you are interviewing for a live-in position, it may concern you if a potential care worker decides to bring boyfriends/girlfriends home to stay. Pre-empt this by mentioning that there are some house rules if the applicant is successful, one of which will include no requests for friends or visitors to stay. If you feel that this is harsh and friends will be allowed to stay, you can leave this open by saying that once they are better known it *may* be possible for some of their friends to be allowed to visit at appropriate times.

- You should discuss all house rules such as no smoking in their room and no drinking, but do so with some positive alternatives such as allowing someone to smoke in the garden.

- Once you have undertaken interviews, you should keep only information received for the person employed. In the event that you have shortlisted anyone you might like to call in case the first choice does not work out, keep these details temporarily. Destroy, by shredding, any other applications and be sure that you tell the unsuccessful candidates that this is your intention. This should be done every time you interview candidates.

- Ensure at the interview stage that you and the applicant are clear on the position of employment and agree whether they will be self-employed or employed. I cannot cover the legal implications of employment status, and would recommend that consumers contact their local office for national insurance regarding guidance on the implications of either status, and also contact their household insurers for the same.

- If you do not wish to be the bearer of bad news in person, then make it clear that you will call the successful candidate by a certain time on a certain day, and that you will write to those who are not being offered the job.

MORE PAPERWORK!

Declaration of eligibility to work

You should also provide a declaration of eligibility to work in the UK and ensure that the applicant signs it.

When approached about consumers privately employing care workers, the Immigration Department states that it is 'the responsibility of anyone paying someone to work in their home to ensure that the worker is legal and if they employ an illegal worker they could be prosecuted'. Remember that ignorance of the law is no defence.

You should ask to see supporting documentation to satisfy yourself that all applicants are legally allowed to work in the UK. I would also suggest that you include any British applicants in your checks. Such an approach will ensure that you are not accused of treating any applicants differently. Insist that you will accept only photographic identification, a move which will act as an additional security measure. In the case of British applicants, still insist on a passport or a new-style photographic driver's licence as proof of identity.

On page 122 is an example of guidance regarding eligibility to work in the UK in order that you can satisfy yourself that an applicant is legally allowed to work. You may use this directly or as a basis to create your own.

You should then satisfy yourself by seeing the documents and countersigning the statement. Retain this for your records as in the event that an applicant has provided falsified information, you can at least show that you acted in good faith and did your best to satisfy yourself that the applicant was legally able to work.

Person specification

I would also recommend that you provide applicants with a person specification if possible (see page 123).

Statement of Eligibility to Work in the UK

In order to ensure compliance with the Asylum and Immigration Act 1996, any offer of employment (even if your status will be self-employed) is made subject to proof of your eligibility to take up paid employment in the UK.

Indicate below, by signing next to the relevant document that you have in your possession, to confirm your eligibility to work in the UK.

■ A passport, which describes you as a British citizen, or as having the right of abode or indefinite leave to remain in the UK, carrying the correct stamp from the Home Office.

....

■ Your birth certificate issued in the UK or in the Republic of Ireland or a certificate of registration or naturalisation as a British citizen, as well as positive proof of identity.

....

■ A passport containing a valid working/holiday visa stamped by the Home Office.

....

■ A passport or identity card issued by a State which is a party to the European Economic Area agreement and which describes you as a national of a State which is a party to that agreement.

....

■ An application registration card issued by the Home Office or a letter issued by the Department for Education and Employment indicating that you have permission to take up the employment on offer, including positive proof of identity (photograph).

....

Person Specification

Job title: Live-in care worker for Mr Green

Role:
- Assistance with aspects of personal care, e.g. bathing, dressing, etc.
- Light cleaning of house
- Cooking
- Laundry duties including ironing
- Shopping
- Driving
- Walking dog daily

Personal capabilities required:
- Good organisational skills including record-keeping
- Ability to work on own initiative
- Self-motivated
- Good communication skills

Experience:
- Must have minimum of one year's direct care experience

Personal characteristics:
- Kind and caring nature
- Trustworthy
- No criminal convictions
- Patient disposition
- Aged 25 or over
- Good command of the English language both written and verbal
- Legal right to work in the UK
- Physically able to undertake the tasks required
- Driver's licence essential (either UK or International or check the position of a foreign licence being valid in the UK)
- Animal lover

Such guidance as to the type of person required will be beneficial to the applicant as well as the consumer. I use the example of a position of live-in care worker, the text for which demonstrates the type of information you might wish to include to satisfy yourself that the applicant is clear about the type of person required.

You should also satisfy yourself that applicants are in good health and therefore completion of a medical enquiry form is advisable (example on page 125).

An application form is *essential* – and a good example is on pages 126–129.

PROCEED WITH CAUTION!

No matter how desperate the need to employ someone, even if the applicant in front of you seems genuine, has a plausible history and is the only applicant you have had, do not offer them the job immediately. There could be problems if their references are not satisfactory.

Don't forget that if you have managed to agree with an umbrella body that they will carry out the CRB checks, then you must also undertake the associated work that comes with that. It is acceptable to let the candidate know that you are very interested in them and that you will be actively speaking to their referees. Give them a time and day by which you will get back to them (being realistic as to the time it will take you to gain references) and ask them how they feel about the position on offer. After all, if you go to the trouble of getting references, you need to make sure that the candidate is interested in the position.

Medical Enquiry Form

Have you:	No	Yes
Had a serious operation within the last five years?		
Suffered a serious injury?		
Received hospital treatment for a mental condition?		
Been dismissed from employment for health reasons?		

Have you ever suffered from or are currently suffering from:

Diabetes	Yes/No		
High blood pressure	Yes/No	Stress induced illness	Yes/No
Asthma	Yes/No	Frequent headaches	Yes/No
Depression	Yes/No	Heart problems	Yes/No
Fainting/dizziness	Yes/No	Back trouble	Yes/No
Psychiatric illness	Yes/No	Ear trouble	Yes/No
Epilepsy/fits	Yes/No	Eye trouble	Yes/No

Do you take medication regularly? Yes/No

If yes, please give details:

....

To the best of my knowledge the information given above is correct. I understand that if I am appointed and this information is inaccurate, I am liable to dismissal.

Signature:..

Print name:............................ Date: ....

Interview date: ....

Interviewer: ....

This application will remain CONFIDENTIAL

Your Personal Information

Surname: ....

First names: ....

Nationality: ....

Do you require a Work Permit? *Yes/No*

Overseas applicants please include the type of work permit you have and the number. British applicants please provide national insurance number: ....

Address: ....

....

Postcode: ....

Daytime contact number: ....

Date of birth: ....

Age: ....**Male/Female** (please circle)

E-mail address: ....

Marital status: ....

Number of children (please include ages): ....

Next of kin (the person you would like contacted in an emergency):

Name: ....

Address: ....

Telephone: ....

Their relationship to you: ....

Work experience:
Please provide details of care experience in the past five years and where gained.

....

....

....

Please provide information regarding any type of training that you have received that is relevant to care work:

....

....

....

Cooking/housekeeping abilities:
How would you describe your ability to cook?
Basic/Fair/Good/Excellent

Do you bake and, if so, describe what type of foods, e.g. bread, cakes, etc.?

....

Do you have a special diet? If so, will this prevent you in any way from dealing with any particular foods? *Yes/No*

If yes, please explain: ....

Are you a smoker? *Yes/No*

Female applicants: are you or could you be pregnant? *Yes/No*

If yes please state your due date:..

Do you have a current clean driver's licence? *Yes/No*

If yes, is your licence from your country of origin or international?

....

What date did you pass your test?......................................

What date does your licence expire?..................................

If you have any driving convictions or have had any accidents within the last five years, please state date of offence/accident and fine imposed/the person blamed for the accident:

....

Can you drive manual or automatic cars or both? (state which):

....

What are your hobbies and interests? ....

....

HAVE YOU EVER COMMITED A CRIMINAL OFFENCE?   *Yes/No*
Please read the Rehabilitation of Offenders Act 1974 below and provide details as requested:

> By virtue of the Rehabilitation of Offenders Act 1974 (Exceptions) Order 1975, the provisions of Section 4.2 of the Rehabilitation of Offenders Act do not apply to any employment which is concerned with the provision of health services and which is of such a kind as to enable the holder to have access to persons in receipt of such services in the course of his normal duties. Please give details of any criminal offences committed, details should include dates and any 'spent' convictions:

HAVE YOU BEEN SUBJECT TO A POLICE CHECK IN THE LAST THREE YEARS INCLUDING COUNTRY OF ORIGIN?   *Yes/No*

If so please give dates and by whom: ....

....

....

DECLARATION

I declare that I have answered the above questions honestly and fully and I am not aware of any physical or mental disability which will or may affect my working capacity.

I realise that any false or incomplete statement on my part will render me liable to dismissal.

SIGNED: .... DATE:.......................

Work History

EMPLOYMENT – PRINT IN BLOCK CAPITALS ONLY
(Please complete this section providing complete employment history within the last three years, starting with the most recent. Please include landline telephone numbers and not mobiles.)

Unless you suggest otherwise, your two most recent employers will be contacted for a reference on your suitability to work as a live-in care giver.

Employer's name, address and phone number	Position you held and dates from until

Please supply the names and telephone numbers of two people willing to confirm your good character.

Name, address and phone number	How long you have known this person for	Relationship to you
1)		
2)		

If they are keen, ask them whether they are actively seeking any other interviews and, if so, when. You could also ask them whether or not they would refrain from going to other scheduled interviews if you were to offer them the job. Their reaction to this question will give you insight as to how much you have impressed them and how much they genuinely want the job.

YOU LIKE AN APPLICANT – WHAT NOW?

You are happy with the applicant's work history, you like them and they have indicated that if the job was offered to them, they would accept. What should be your next step?

You should take up references as soon as possible. When speaking to referees, explain that the position applied for is one caring for a potentially vulnerable individual and ensure that you ask them the following questions regarding the applicant:

- In what capacity do they know them and for how long?

- Have they ever known them in a position of trust?

- Do they know of any physical or mental reason why they should not care for a vulnerable individual?

- What did their duties involve when working for the referee?

- Would they be happy for the applicant to care for a member of their family if the reference did not relate to such a position?

- Are they reliable or did they take much sick leave?

- What is their personality like, e.g. has the referee ever seen them moody or aggressive with co-workers or were they popular?

■ What was their reason for leaving?

■ How long did they work for the referee?

All of the answers must be cross-referenced with the notes you made based on the applicant's answers to the interview questions. You also need to keep an open mind when it comes to references and maintain a realistic attitude. You are not looking for three glowing references - you are more interested in being told the truth. A referee might say: 'She was OK' which isn't exactly earth shattering! But check that this ties up with the work history, reliability, etc. as per your notes.

OFFERING THEM THE JOB

If you decide to offer an applicant the job, do so verbally and follow this up formally with a letter.

You should keep a file with the successful care worker's application form as this will have the contact details for their next of kin in case they are ever ill. You do not necessarily need to take references in writing, but you should keep all comments and notes taken just in case a problem arises.

THE LAST WORD

There are many variables to be aware of when employing people and many things are taken for granted when one recruits care workers on a weekly basis as I did. To include everything on this subject would be an impossible task.

If privately employing, consumers may choose to have a close relative or friend to help oversee the situation or undertake the process, but it will ultimately be the consumer who will face problems including being left without care if the worker is taken ill, or being trapped with second-rate care if things don't go right.

So what if problems do arise and those involved can't face the recruitment process a second time?

I am going to suggest a compromise – that consumers register with a service provider (not an employment agency). I will explain why.

If a consumer registers with a service provider, some will charge a registration fee to be placed on their books. Consumers can then call as and when they require assistance. Registration fees are often under £100 which is a small price to pay for the reassurance it will provide.

If an individual has recruited privately for a few hours' assistance daily and the care worker is absent, the service provider may be unable to send someone for the same number of hours or the same length of time as the private person would have attended. However, they will be able to get someone to pop in and do the basics and will charge accordingly. The hourly rate will undoubtedly be higher than that of the private person, but it is likely to be short term and the alternative is no care at all.

If a consumer has recruited privately for a live-in care worker, then the problems become greater if the worker is ill or needs to leave suddenly. But if a consumer is registered with a live-in service provider, they can be asked to cover breaks taken by the private care worker and can be called upon in the event of an emergency.

9

Arranging Care Home Services

If a care home is the chosen care solution start by taking the following steps.

1. CHOOSE A SELECTION OF HOMES

Draw up a list of prospective homes.

2. REQUEST INFORMATION

Make contact with potential homes and request their brochures. Even if a care home has been highly recommended don't be tempted to just make an appointment to visit. Ask the home whether their brochure includes fees and, if self- or part-funding, and ask for a copy of the contract. If you have access to a solicitor, then it is advisable, as with any legal document, to have the contract examined.

If the home states that fees or a contract are not included in the initial enquiry pack, be polite but firm and insist that they send you this information. Explain that you do not want to waste valuable planning time and need all important documentation now in order that you can determine whether you wish to take your enquiry further. If you have not obtained a copy, also ask them to include their most recent inspection report. Any reluctance on a provider's part to furnish you with any of these documents can be reported to the local CSCI.

If the care is likely to be paid for by the local authority, and assuming the choice of home is one that they agree to, then they will already have a contract with the provider. You should still ask for the terms of residency as you will need to know what is *not included* in the fees paid by the local authority, as the cared-for individual will be liable for these.

Ask the care home how soon they will send the brochure and take the name of the person you are speaking to. This way, if the brochure does not arrive by the specified time, you can contact the home again. Upon receipt of a brochure read the content thoroughly.

3. VISIT

Once a consumer is happy with the costs and conditions of a selection of care homes, this is the stage at which to make appointments to visit.

4. ASK MEANINGFUL QUESTIONS AND MAKE OBSERVATIONS

In Part 2 the minimum care standards in respect of care homes are listed and you should highlight those that you feel are important before visiting homes.

Later in this chapter I provide questions that you could ask prospective care homes. Next to each question is the number of the 'care standard' corresponding to that question. I strongly encourage you to cross-reference them. Familiarity with the standards is very important. For example, some advertisements for care homes state how consumers can bring their own furniture to the home as if this is a *unique* selling point for that establishment. Yet it is an *obligation* on the part of the home to allow individuals to bring a selection of personal effects in adherence to the standards.

Know your consumer rights by referring to the standards and you will be able to judge a home more effectively – you will know where they are going above the standards and when they are doing the bare minimum required of them.

When visiting a home it is likely that you will be invited at quieter times and so you will need to ask many questions to find out about the home's compliance with certain standards rather than witness them first hand. It would be a good idea though to ask a home whether you could join them for lunch. This will enable you to get some valuable insight and would not only give you an opportunity to taste the food, but you could also see the presentation at meals, observe the staff interaction and above all gain a valuable opportunity to talk to those individuals already using the service. Given that the option of trial visits is included in the care standards I doubt a home would be shocked at such a request. If you are arranging services in a professional capacity such as a social worker, I would still recommend this as good practice.

What activities are available?

As mentioned above, there are many questions to ask and

observations I suggest you make, but there is one point I would like to raise in isolation. When you visit a care home, you need to know what leisure and recreational activities are available both inside and outside of the home. You must insist on specific answers, not woolly suggestions that a home sometimes provides activities.

There is no doubt that many care homes have programmes of activities, but many activity programmes within the brochures I saw really were *non-activities*. I therefore want to cover this point in a little more detail.

A person may live in a care home for a significant number of years and to sit looking at the same four walls, going through the same routine, is not going to be conducive to mental, physical or spiritual well-being.

The standards require care homes to have programmes of activity, but I fear that some homes struggle to be creative for many reasons, such as a shortage of staff or a lack of transport.

A service must consider an individual's complete well-being. The Commission felt that leisure activity was of enough importance to be included in the standards. The problem, however, is that there is no guidance about the level or type of activities or whether homes should have access to transport for external activities. Care homes for this reason are able to determine the level and quality of activities for themselves and I fear that many run non-activities, that is things that do not require a great deal of effort.

Activities arranged within care homes vary enormously but they should be appropriate to the consumer group and be something that needs to be arranged!

Some homes run reminiscence therapy and when short-term memory is severely damaged an individual can benefit from this type of activity. Immediate questions requiring short-term answers such as 'Where have you just been Betty?' are no longer the focus – instead individuals are given an opportunity to remember what they *can* of bygone days. But for those with unaffected mental capacities discussing the old times with anyone who is interested should be spontaneous and so would not suit them. I also think that the word 'therapy' can be misleading.

Playing cards is something that I am sure many individuals in a care home could do between themselves with minimal supervision. It is difficult to see how playing cards can be classed as an activity provided by the home, unless workers are playing with the group.

One leisure activity timetable received from a care home stated that on Tuesday and Thursday, Mass is held, and on Monday and Wednesday, bingo. While I do not dispute that bingo is definitely an activity, I do not understand how Mass can be considered one. Mass is the following of an individual's spiritual and religious beliefs and is the worship of God – it is not just an 'activity'.

What about the quality of external leisure and recreation?

I have experienced at first-hand individuals who are bundled into minibuses and driven for miles for no more than a cup of tea before being brought back home again. I don't think that this is meaningful activity.

> **GOOD FOR THEM**
>
> A 92-year-old lady had teased her grand-daughter for months saying that she wanted to ride pillion on the back of the family quad bike, but the challenge was never taken seriously. However following the death of her cat, the lady was cheered up by a suggestion from her grand-daughter that she honour the request. The 'ladies' took a fairly slow half-hour spin around the countryside and while the older lady claimed the trip didn't make her any less sad about the loss of her kitty, she said that the experience had reminded her that life goes on and that you are never too old to do something new. Her grand-daughter said that her gran's spirit of adventure never failed to amaze her and the spontaneity of the change to the daily routine following such a sad event had brought a real twinkle to her gran's eye. The revelation of what the ladies had done brought mixed reactions from the rest of the family, but the grand-daughter felt that the pleasure it brought far outweighed the potential risks.
>
> **What do you think?**

What would be meaningful activity both off and on site?

- Onsite activities such as a sing-along would be ideal.

- In residential homes where consumers are a little more able, why not pull back the sofas and have a dancing competition?

- There could be a video club set up where all those interested take a vote on the film for the evening.

- Other ideas that are great fun for all ages are activities such as giant indoor skittles.

- For those perhaps a little more fit and able, what about themed evenings or staging a show? Consumers could be involved in

dressmaking, props and promotion. This is especially beneficial to those with learning difficulties.

■ Outside the home, there are the theatre, cinema, art galleries
and exhibitions.

■ Or how about visits to the local flea market or, for those willing
to get up early enough, the occasional Sunday morning car-
boot sale?

I appreciate that there are limitations, but I ran a residential home
from 1992 for two years. During that time we had countless
barbeques to which friends and family were always invited. This is
something which I know many places refuse to do for fear of
being sued for giving someone food poisoning, but progressive
care providers will find ways of ensuring that fear does not ruin
the quality of life for consumers!

We took trips to the seaside to enjoy fish and chips and ice cream,
and theatre visits were the norm. The majority of the consumers
of the service, while mobile, suffered with some form of
dementia. Yet we never had any problems with the outings and
they only served to ensure that those staying at the home were
happy, contented and felt they were receiving value for money.
The care workers also felt fulfilled because they were making a
difference.

WHY?

Q: Why do so few people take holidays once they have moved into a
residential or nursing care setting?

A: Because few people are aware of the fact that there are lots of holiday
organisations specifically catering to the less able-bodied traveller *and*

because many people take the attitude that, once they are in a care home, that is where they will stay and no longer challenge themselves to new experiences, and *equally* because care homes do not encourage them to do so *nor* does society as a whole. Yet there are many insurance companies who provide travel insurance for older or disabled people as well as those with ill-health. There would also be many care workers who, if given the opportunity to accompany individuals on a trip, would be delighted to do so.

Questions and observations

I accept that some of the following questions may already have been answered in a brochure but let us assume you don't already know the answers:

Key questions

- Does the consumer have to get up or go to bed by a certain time each day? (*Standard 12*)

- Does the consumer have to eat meals at a certain time? (*Standard 12*)

- Does the consumer have to do socially what everybody else is doing? (*Standard 13*)

- Does the consumer have to take baths at certain times? (*Standard 12*)

What else you need to know

- How many vacancies does the home have and how long have the rooms been available?

- What qualifications do the care workers have? (*Standard 28*)

- What induction process do workers go through, including the topics covered? (*Standard 30*)

- How thorough are the recruitment processes? (*Standard 29*)

- What qualification does the registered manager hold? (*Standard 28*)

- Does the home arrange for annual reviews of medication? (See 'GP' in Chapter 3)

- Can an individual bring personal effects such as an easy chair? (*Standards 14 and 24*)

- Are bedrooms shared? (*Standard 23*)

- Can you see the complaints and compliments file? (*Standard 16*)

- How involved are consumers in choosing meals? (*Standard 32*)

- Has the home had any cases of service users suffering malnutrition? (*Standard 15*)

- Where do they buy their food? (*Standard 15*)

- How many meals a day are provided? (*Standard 15*)

- Are snacks made available between meals? (*Standard 15*)

- Do consumers have an opportunity to give feedback in a constructive way, e.g. residents' meetings? (*Standards 14 and 32*)

- What recreational facilities are available? (*Standard 12*)

- Are there specific visiting times for friends and family? (*Standard 13*)

■ Can friends/family have tea or a meal at the home? If so, is there an associated cost?

■ Are there external links to the community, e.g. opportunities to go to the local church? (*Standard 13*)

■ If incontinence aids are used, do consumers have to pay extra?

If a home honours a consumer's rights and understands their own obligations, then this is what they are being paid to do. If they go beyond their obligations, then consumers will be getting real value for money.

Nearly all of the questions I list are in relation to minimum standards and therefore they are not unrealistic or unreasonable by any means.

If you receive the most basic answers to the simplest of questions, or worse still the person showing you around does not know the answers, then you may need to consider your choice of home more carefully. It could be that the member of staff you are talking to is new or inexperienced, but that in itself should raise doubt. If potential custom is important to this care provider, why allow a new or inexperienced worker to deal with you?

Any person showing you around a care or group home should be familiar with providing this type of information to potential consumers. The questions asked at the outset are simple ones that will give a feel for the home. There will undoubtedly be additional questions should you wish to take your enquiries further, at which point the finer detail of the contract becomes important, as does the matter of insurance.

Contracts, insurance and key policies and procedures

I am unable to cover contracts thoroughly because there will be thousands of different ones. But the standards do cover the main points and by reading contracts through you will see if issues such as insurance are covered. If this is not the case, then you must raise the matter and ensure that you get an answer on liability in writing. You need to know if the home's insurance covers your personal effects in the event of theft by a care worker, other resident or fire damage.

Another way to be satisfied that a home is right is by checking key policies. This will highlight what sort of action the home will take in any given circumstance covered by the policy. Policy and procedure should be readily available and easily accessible.

Abuse

You also need to know whether there have been any accusations of abuse of any kind within the last three years and the outcome of any investigations. Question should include:

- Whether accusations of abuse are taken seriously (see Chapter 5).

- Whether the care home has a good and robust policy in place to protect all parties (remember, abuse is not always care worker to consumer – it can be the other way around).

- Whether they fulfil their legal obligation to notify relevant authorities such as Social Services and the CSCI of accusations.

- Whether issues are concluded speedily.

■ Whether outcomes are achieved or investigations are forgotten half way through (believe me – it happens!).

I'm not suggesting you be allowed to have access to details of specific abuse cases (if any), but you need to get a general feel for the situation.

Complaints and compliments

You should also request to see the complaints and compliments file and you should welcome any information pertaining to day-to-day complaints of any nature. Recording of complaints will prove that the care home is approachable and has a good method of recording information. Of course you will want to see some proof of resolutions of complaints, even if this is just a verbal explanation.

Any care home that states they have had no complaints (not necessarily abuse complaints) in the past three years is not being honest or realistic. Any gripes, no matter how small, should be noted in writing. By doing so, the home's management is showing they will take seriously all matters raised.

Inspection reports

The inspection report for each establishment should show how many serious complaints a service has received, so you can cross-reference answers. The problem in part is that you and the inspectors are reliant on the care home's honesty.

What current consumers have to say

It is always worth having informal chats with current consumers of the service to get the low-down, on the understanding that what they say will go no further. To be given the opportunity to do so is covered by the standards. In the event that a consumer of the service discloses any information that causes you concern regarding their treatment by the home you must report those concerns to the CSCI. I would *not recommend* that you tackle issues directly with the home, no matter how strongly you may feel about a situation.

Other observations

Other observations you make could include but are not limited to:

■ How do care workers interact with current consumers? Do they provide unhurried assistance or do they look over-worked?

■ Do they ask individuals quietly whether they would like the bathroom, or shout loud enough for everyone to hear?

■ Is there an unpleasant odour in the home or is it fresh and inviting?

■ Are there homely signs such as fresh flowers or pets of any description?

■ Do consumers look unkempt or wearing dirty clothes, or does everybody look well cared for and happy?

5. TRIAL VISIT

No matter how thorough your investigations are into the services offered, the only real test of whether a care home is suitable for a consumer is for them to undertake a trial visit.

You will need to establish whether homes will charge for such a visit and it may be that the chosen home does not have immediate vacancies.

If time permits and even if there are no immediate vacancies, ask if it is possible for the consumer to spend a couple of days at the care home and return to their own home at night. This way, there will be no waiting on a list for a care home that isn't right. A waiting list is not necessarily an indication that the home is ideal.

Having visited, if the home is the right one but there are no vacancies and a consumer's condition is such that they cannot manage alone, then perhaps live-in care should be considered as an interim solution until a place becomes available.

Whichever way you handle things from here, you are well on your way to making a fully-informed choice of care home.

> **REMEMBER**
> The only stupid question is the one not asked.

10

Arranging Domiciliary Care Services

As previously mentioned, unlike arranging a care home, choosing domiciliary care is less tangibly quantifiable and this can make the decision-making process so much harder. You can see if a care home is pleasant and you can talk to fellow consumers, but your investigations in respect of domiciliary care need to be somewhat more thorough and the questions asked specific enough to get the answers required.

If you wish to investigate the domiciliary care option further, then the following five-point process should be used whatever type of domiciliary help is required. I have made it clear whether these questions are relevant only to daily or live-in type care, because there are a few differences.

I have not indicated if the questions are excluded for employment agencies. This is because, as you know, the Commission exclude agencies from certain parts of some of the standards, and to try to indicate this within the questions section could become messy. I also think it would be in your interests to ask the questions and hear for yourself the answers from an agency as to whether they are included or excluded from compliance, as their response may make you think in greater depth about whether they are the right care choice for your situation.

You may need to refer to the overview of the standards to get a clear understanding of which do not apply to agencies.

How to get started:

1. CHOOSE A SELECTION OF COMPANIES

You should know ways in which to access services and should have determined some companies which interest you based on location, recommendation, availability of service, etc.

2. REQUEST INFORMATION

Make contact with potential contenders and obtain their brochures. Upon receipt of the literature read it thoroughly. Even if a domiciliary company has been highly recommended, you should still follow this guidance.

Ask the company whether the brochure includes fees and, if self- or part-funded, ask for a copy of the contract. If you have the means to access a solicitor then it is advisable, as with any legal document, to have the contract looked over by an individual qualified to do so.

If fees or a contract are not included, insist on copies. Explain that you do not want to waste valuable planning time and need all important documentation in order that you can determine whether you wish to take your enquiry further. Ask that a copy of their most recent inspection report is also enclosed.

Any reluctance on a provider's part to provide these documents should be reported to CSCI, details of which can be found in Chapter 1.

If care is to be paid for by the local authority they will already have a contract with the provider. However, you should still ask for a list of their terms of service and a list of requirements or similar document indicating the consumer's responsibilities. You will also need to know what is not included in the fees paid by the local authority as the consumer will be liable for extras.

Ask how long it will take them to send the brochure and take down the name of the person you are speaking to. If the brochure does not arrive by the specified time, you can contact the provider again and you will have a named individual who can relate to your query.

3. ARRANGE AN ASSESSMENT

If you are happy with the costs and conditions of a selection of service providers/agencies, and you have seen a copy of their inspection reports, make appointments for them to visit the consumer at home.

4. ASK MEANINGFUL QUESTIONS AND MAKE OBSERVATIONS

An assessment is required as part of the NMCS and includes both *agencies* and *service providers* in its compliance. Some inspectors allow employment agencies to conduct assessments over the telephone rather than in person. I can think of little benefit to consumers of such an arrangement, only convenience for the agency. My advice would be to consider using only a company which undertakes a care needs assessment in person, not via the telephone.

I would suggest that before an assessment is undertaken, you look through the standards and highlight those areas you feel are important to you so you can discuss those aspects in depth with the assessor. Do keep in mind that if it is an employment agency that is assessing you, not all of the standards will be applicable, so there will be a limited amount of information that they will require.

You should know your rights in relation to the NMCS in order that you can see whether the organisation is exceeding the standards expected of them or scraping by with the minimum. You can then use your knowledge of the standards and ask lots of questions pertaining to them.

Some of the following questions may have already been answered in the initial care provider/agency brochure and some may not.

Key questions and observations

Assuming you don't already know the answers, key questions should include:

- Do the workers, both office and care workers, undergo Criminal Record Bureau checks and, if so, are these completed prior to them having access to consumers' records or to placing them in the home? (*Standard 17*)

- Some allowances are made by the CSCI for well-supervised providers of care to undertake a preliminary check of care worker suitability and place those workers *before* their completed full CRB check is received, as long as certain safeguards are in place. If a care provider or agency states that such allowances have been made for their company, you will need to satisfy yourself that such allowances are worthy of the safeguards in place. An example of a safety measure *should in all cases* include the need to run a POVA first check. So if a company claims that the CSCI has made an allowance on the placement of workers prior to receipt of their full CRB disclosure, they should be able to explain to you what a POVA first entails. You should also be aware that if a care provider is placing care staff prior to receipt of a full disclosure, they are obliged to notify consumers of this fact.

■ Do they provide induction training for care workers? (*Standard 19*).

■ What does the induction cover? (*Standard 19*)

■ During training, do care staff undertake tasks that they are assessed on, or do they simply watch videos? (*Standard 19*)

When questioned, some organisations think it acceptable to place an inexperienced care worker in front of a television to watch a video on safe manual handling – and call it training! During my time as a qualified manual handling trainer, I would never allow a care worker to set foot in a consumer's home until they had demonstrated that they provide safe handling of individuals and did so by having a mock home set-up within a training centre (in my case the training centre was a house) with a bed, hoist, chair, commode, etc. Care workers hoisted or moved one of their colleagues to prove that they had understood the concepts of safe practice. This is a basic principle to ensure safety and so do ask questions on training with these points in mind.

Questions you should also ask

■ What qualifications does the person training the care workers hold? (*Standard 20*)

- What qualifications do the care workers have or are working towards? (*Standard 20*)

- If a care worker is preparing meals, do they have basic food hygiene training?

- What qualifications does the office team have? (*Standard 20*)

- What qualification does the registered manager hold? (*Standard 20*)

- What recruitment processes do they take workers through? (*Standard 17*)

- Does someone within the company speak to all care worker referees? (*Standard 17*)

- Do they accept open references? (*Standard 17*)

- Daily care: how early can the care workers visit consumers? (*Standard 6*)

- Daily care: how late can they work? (*Standard 6*)

- Can they undertake any household cleaning tasks?

- Can they do shopping?

- If they have one, are they allowed to take consumers in their car or can they drive the consumer's car?

- Have there been incidences of care workers forgetting to visit a consumer, or office staff forgetting to schedule a visit? If so, how was it dealt with?

- How is last-minute sickness dealt with? (*Standard 6*)

- How do consumers contact the organisation outside of office hours? (*Standard 4*)

- Is the assessor qualified to assess handling needs? (*Standard 2*)

- If necessary, can the organisation recommend any equipment that would help the consumer and the care worker? (*Standard 2*)

- What qualifications does the assessor have to enable them to make such recommendations?

- How does the organisation monitor the service provided? (*Standards 21 and 26*)

- Will consumers receive visits on a regular basis from the management team? (*Standards 21 and 27*)

- Live-in: will care workers take consumers out and about?

- Live-in: can care workers take consumers on holiday and if so who pays for what?

- Live-in: if consumer and worker go to the cinema or somewhere similar, who pays the entrance fee for the care worker?

I will discuss further the last three points which are very important as they are in effect activities and are not covered by the standards for *domiciliary care agencies.*

Activities and holidays
Domiciliary service providers, just as much as care homes, should be encouraging their live-in workers to provide meaningful leisure activities. There are no care standards relevant to leisure activities for domiciliary care, but it would be good practice.

If it has been assessed as safe for a consumer to go out then service providers should encourage care workers to arrange outings, otherwise there is still a danger that the consumer's own four walls will be stared at all day.

There are many forms of transport such as wheelchair adapted taxis that can be called upon to facilitate outings, and the train services (with advance notice) can also accommodate the needs of wheelchair users, as can buses with no advanced notice required.

If a consumer likes visiting art galleries or the cinema or theatre, then have the care worker call them in advance in order to ascertain whether a fee is payable for the care worker's access. Some establishments require a person who is elderly or disabled to pay their own admission, but will allow a care worker to accompany them free.

If the care worker's access needs to be paid, each company will have its own rules as to whose responsibility this is, so consumers should clarify the point. Care workers may hold a view that differs from the care provider.

If holidays are taken, not only will consumers need to confirm who pays, but also ensure that, if using a service provider, the provider has notified their insurers and that the worker and consumer will still receive relevant protection under the organisation's insurance cover.

If a consumer has a handling need, you must discuss any plans for holidays with the service provider in advance. They may wish to make their own enquiries, with health and safety in mind, as to the suitability of chosen accommodation.

There are many travel organisations and independent holiday homes catering for the less able traveller. Details and websites for these can be found through any Internet search engine.

> **Note**
>
> Nearly all of the questions I suggest you raise with an assessor are in relation to the NMCS and any person carrying out assessments should be used to providing this information to potential consumers.
>
> The questions you ask at the outset are simple questions that will give you a feel for the company initially. There will no doubt be further questions in the event that you wish to take the matter to the next stage.

Contracts and insurance

The issue of the contract will then become very important, as will points such as insurance. I am unable to cover contracts thoroughly because there will be thousands of different variations. But the standards do cover contracts in general and issues such as insurance.

If insurance is not covered in the contract or you are unsure as to the liability of either party, then raise the question with the assessor and insist on an answer about responsibility in writing. This becomes especially important to those in receipt of live-in care, given the many situations that could arise resulting in a claim.

Ask questions such as:

- Who would be responsible for paying the excess insurance if a care worker had an accident when driving the consumer's car?

- What if a care worker accidentally broke something of value? Would the company or the care worker pay for a replacement item, or does the consumer have to accept that accidents happen and claim on their own household insurance?

You may think that such questions have straightforward answers, but this is not necessarily the case. For example, if a care worker is told that in the event of an accident in a consumer's vehicle they are financially responsible, many care workers would simply refuse to take on positions where they have to drive. Of course, it may be different if it has been agreed with the consumer, the care provider and the worker that workers can use the car in their own time. But what if an accident occurs in the course of a worker's duties, such as driving a consumer to their workplace or an appointment? As you can see, it can be a hard subject to tackle and not one you want to be negotiating *after* a problem has arisen.

Household insurance claims can be just as contentious because there is naturally going to be an increased risk of breakages, spillages and wear and tear with an extra person in the home. Prudent organisations should advise consumers to contact their insurer and notify them of the fact that you have domiciliary care workers as most care organisations will not take responsibility for day-to-day household damages.

None of the issues raised on this topic should be new for an assessor and they should be able to confidently answer any basic questions you raise. But with the complexity of insurance, their employers may recommend that queries are directed to management.

Finally on the subject of insurance, consumers do need to be sure that their household cover has public liability insurance that will extend to care workers. For example, if a wheelchair user accidentally ran over a care worker's foot and broke their toe then who could be held responsible?

> **REMEMBER**
> The private employment of care staff really does put the onus on the consumer and care worker to be crystal clear about responsibility.

Key policies and procedures

To satisfy yourself that a company is the right one do not be afraid to ask to see key policies. This will help you to establish what sort of action is taken in given situations. Policy and procedure should be readily available and easily accessible. You should ask the organisation to send key policy documents with the assessor at that stage. They can always be read after the assessor has gone and a decision can be made based on all the facts, including whether the assessor seemed to have confidence in the company.

Abuse

As with care homes, you will need to know whether there have been any accusations of abuse of any kind within the last three years and the outcome of any investigations. You should look into the following:

- Whether accusations of abuse are taken seriously (see Chapter 5).

- Whether the care provider has a good and robust policy in place to protect both the consumer and employee (remember, abuse is not always care worker to consumer – it can be the other way around).

- Whether the company fulfils its legal obligation to notify relevant authorities such as Social Services and the CSCI.

- Whether issues are concluded speedily.

- Whether outcomes are achieved or investigations are forgotten half way through (believe me, it happens!).

You should not be allowed to have access to details of specific abuse cases (if any), but you need to get a general feel for the situation.

Complaints and compliments

You can also ask that the assessor to bring some samples from their complaints and compliments file and assure them that you will welcome any information pertaining to day-to-day complaints of any nature. Of course they will need to omit details of the complainant or seek permission of the people complimenting the service to share it with a third party. You should question whether permission was sought or observe whether they have removed the writer's personal details such as their name and address. The handling of this matter will speak volumes about the organisation.

The recording of complaints will prove that the company is approachable and has a good method of retaining information. You will want some proof of the resolution of complaints, even if this is just a verbal explanation.

Any company that states they have had no complaints (not necessarily abuse complaints) in the past three years is not being honest or realistic. Any gripes, no matter how small, should be recorded and by doing so the organisation's management are showing they take seriously any matter raised.

The inspection report for each agency should show how many serious complaints a service has received so you can cross-reference their answer. Of course you and the inspectors are reliant on the honesty of the company, or indeed their organisational skills in respect of logging complaints.

What current users have to say

It's always worth having informal chats with current users of the service provider/agency to get the low-down, on the understanding that what they say will go no further. Most care companies, if they are providing a good level of care, will not find it difficult to find a willing consumer to vouch for them.

As with care homes, in the event that a current consumer of a service discloses any information regarding their treatment by the company and such a disclosure concerns you then report your concerns to the CSCI. I would *not recommend* that you tackle issues directly with the company, no matter how strongly you may feel about the situation.

Other observations

Other observations you make could include but are not limited to the following:

- How does the assessor refer other consumers of the service? Do they speak fondly of them but with discretion or do they use names in the assumption that you won't know the person they are discussing?

- Does the assessor appear positive and convinced of the service they are promoting?

- Do they tell you of any individual approaches that may indicate a personal touch, such as the service provider/agency sending birthday cards to consumers and care workers?

- You may wish to ask the assessor how many care staff the company employs and how many customers they care for.

- Ask whether the care can be provided on a trial basis initially.

5. ARRANGE CARE ON A TRIAL BASIS

No matter how thorough your investigations into services, the only real test of whether a company is suitable is to undertake care on a trial basis.

- If choosing live-in care, I would suggest that two weeks is sufficient time to establish whether an individual will be comfortable with the service.

- In the event that daily care is chosen, then a month is more likely to be a good length of time to enable a fully-informed choice of service provider/agency to be made.

REMEMBER
The only stupid question is the one not asked.

11

When the Inspector Calls

The greatest protection for care consumers is the mandatory registration of care services within the UK. No service can operate without being registered with their relevant organisation – which in England is currently the CSCI. Once registered to provide a service, monitoring of the provision of care is undertaken thereafter.

Up until 2006, inspection frequency was as follows:

- Care homes had *at least* one announced inspection and one unannounced inspection every 12 months.

- Domiciliary care agencies had *at least* one announced inspection every 12 months.

During the inspection organisations were monitored against the NMCS and marked with a number according to whether:

- They failed to meet the standard – 1.
- They partially met the standard – 2.
- They fully met a standard – 3.
- They exceeded a standard – 4.
- The standard was not one against which an organisation was inspected, such as where an agency only introduces workers – X.

This process of inspection was used for just a few years and has now been replaced with the following.

KEY INSPECTIONS

This is the most thorough type of inspection when an inspector looks at all aspects of a service.

- They won't usually tell the care provider in advance when they will visit.

- Before the inspection, they look at all the information held on a service – such as information about concerns, complaints or allegations, incidents, previous inspections and reports – to see how well the service has performed in the past and how much they have improved it since the last inspection.

- Inspectors will look at what managers of the service tell them about how they think their service is doing.

- They will also gain the views of people who use the service, their families and any professionals involved. This may be through talking to them or sending out surveys.

- The assessment of the quality of a service is based on all this information, plus an inspector's own observations during their visit.

- Assessment is discussed with those running the care organisation.

Frequency of visits

- The frequency of inspection will depend on how the CSCI judge quality of service, but every new service will receive a key inspection in its first year.

- Key inspections are major assessments of the quality of a service and any risk that it might present.

- Once the CSCI has determined the quality of a service the following frequency of inspections will apply.

Star rating	Frequency
3 star *** (Excellent)	One key inspection at least once every three years
2 star ** (Good)	One key inspection at least once every two years
1 star * (Adequate)	One key inspection at least once a year
0 star (Poor)	Two key inspections a year

If the CSCI is considering enforcement action they may undertake more key inspections. In addition to key inspections they may also carry out random or thematic inspection visits.

RANDOM INSPECTIONS

These shorter inspections take place if there is a specific issue with a service that the CSCI needs to follow up. They happen *in addition* to the key inspection.

- An inspector might be following up information about a complaint or allegation, or seeing what progress an organisation is making on an issue arising from an earlier inspection. They may also visit if there has been a change in manager or changes have been made to a service.

- Sometimes they may visit a 'good' service as part of their random checks.

- Random inspections will *usually be unannounced.*

Frequency

- These inspections are called 'random' because they may happen at any time.

- The CSCI wants to reassure people who use services and the public that they are monitoring the care people receive.

THEMATIC INSPECTIONS

These will focus on national or regional issues. For example, inspectors might look at how medication is managed, or have a theme on nutrition, or they may look at the development of specific types of services in an area.

Their findings will go towards a national report and the CSCI will ask a care provider's permission to use their service as an example if they identify an area of really good practice, or where great improvements have been made in a specific area.

The first thematic inspections were undertaken in 2006, when information provided to people to help them make choices when they are moving into a care home were looked at.

Frequency

Inspectors intend to continue to inspect a sample of care services against specific themes, with the aim of focusing on up to two themes per year.

ANNUAL SERVICE REVIEW

An annual service review is a report that CSCI writes for *good or excellent services* **that have not had a key inspection in the past year.**

- It does *not* include a visit to the service, but is a summary of all the information that the CSCI has received from the organisation or that the inspectors have gathered through their regulatory role since the last key inspection.

- An annual service review is usually carried out six weeks after an organisation has sent the CSCI their annual quality assurance assessment (*AQAA*).

- The annual service review is how inspectors assure themselves, and the public, that the quality of a service has not changed since the last key inspection.

Assessing quality

If the review shows that a service is still performing as well as it was at the last key inspection, the inspection plans for that service will not be changed. For example, if a service was good and a key inspection was not due for another year then it would be another year before a key inspection was undertaken. However, if the AQAA shows that the quality of a service has deteriorated then the CSCI will *probably* visit an organisation to do an inspection sooner and write a report on what they find.

The report

- Organisations will have the chance to comment on the factual accuracy of the draft annual service review in the same way as they have with other reports.

- The annual service review is a public document available from the CSCI website.

WHAT TO EXPECT DURING AN INSPECTION

It is worth knowing what an inspection is like, who inspectors are and how they involve people who use services, as you might be called upon to share your views.

About inspectors

- CSCI inspectors are experienced social care or healthcare workers. Many have been senior managers of care services, have a background in nursing or social work or hold another professional qualification. They are trained in inspection and work to an agreed code of conduct.

- When an inspector undertakes their duty, they should be professional and courteous at all times. Each inspector should carry their ID and authorisation card.

- If a care provider feels that an inspector has not behaved fairly, they should talk to the local CSCI office or make a formal complaint to the Commission.

What to expect

- A site visit will usually last one day but may be more depending on the size and nature of the service and the issues arising.

- Inspectors use a range of methods to gather evidence about how well a service meets the needs of the people who use it.

This includes talking to people who use the service and observing their interaction with staff where appropriate.

- They also look at the environment and facilities provided and check records such as care plans and risk assessments.

- For key inspection visits they will concentrate on how well the service performs against the outcomes for the 'key' national minimum standards for each type of service and how the users experience the service.

- The key standards are shown in inspection reports.

OUTCOMES

Each set of minimum standards has a desired outcome. For example, in the national minimum standards for care homes, Standards 1–6 are designed with a particular outcome in mind, in this case that all potential and current users of services have access to sufficient information pertaining to the service into which they will buy or have already bought.

The inspection will explore whether a service offers people who use it the lifestyle, choice, participation and appropriate health or social care to meet their needs.

The inspector will look at evidence to help them assess how people experience the service. They will spend time with people who receive the service and will also speak to those working within the organisation.

They will clarify any points the inspection raises with the manager, and discuss with them any plans to develop and improve the service. The inspector will let the organisation know what their report is likely to say before they leave, and clarify any areas that require immediate attention.

The CSCI uses the term 'outcome' to describe the impact of the service on the person using it, and the national minimum standards set out the desired outcomes for each of the standards.

For example, for care homes for older people there is a standard about information (*Standard 1*). If the service meets this standard, the outcome for the person using the service is defined as:

> *Prospective service users have the information they need to make an informed choice about where to live.*

The standards are grouped into *outcome headings*, which highlight aspects of individuals' lives identified as most important to people who use services. The outcomes vary slightly depending on the type of service. For example, the outcomes groups for care homes for older people are:

- Choice of home
- Health and personal care
- Daily life and social activities
- Complaints and protection
- Environment
- Staffing
- Management and administration.

The CSCI will look at how well care providers meet the standards they think are the most important for the service at the time of inspection which are called *key standards*. They will make a judgment for each outcome heading, *not* individual standards.

The judgments are:

- Poor
- Adequate
- Good
- Excellent.

The judgments they make will determine the star rating of the service.

HOW THEY INVOLVE THE PEOPLE WHO USE SERVICES

The CSCI thinks it is important that the views and experiences of people using services, and those of their friends, families and advocates, be taken into account when reaching a judgment on the quality of a service and they have reviewed how they do this.

Here are some of the things they will look at when inspecting a service.

Case tracking

This is a way of inspecting that helps the CSCI to look at services from the point of view of the people who use them. They look at the experiences of a sample group including how they arrived at needing the service, what choices they had in choosing the service and their experience of receiving the service.

Inspectors are now using new methods that include better surveys and an *observational tool* called a *Short Observation Framework for Inspections* (SOFI). This helps inspectors to observe care home residents with communication difficulties. Further information can be obtained from the CSCI website.

Involving 'experts by experience' in inspections

People who have direct experience of using social care services, including carers, are often good judges of whether another service is working well for the people using it. So, people who are experienced in receiving a service help the CSCI with some of the adult services inspections and these people are called *experts by experience*. They may accompany inspectors for some of the time they visit a service. Their feedback will help the Commission with their judgments and will be reflected in their reports.

After an inspection

This review was introduced in 2007 for *good and excellent services only* **instead of a** *key inspection.*

Every year, around the anniversary of the first key inspection, the CSCI will review all the information they have about a service. They will look especially at new information or changes that provider organisations or others have told them about. This will include things like:

- changes in the registered provider or manager
- changes or improvements to the service
- concerns or complaints about the service
- the main findings of random or thematic inspections
- whether providers have sent their annual quality assurance assessment.

The CSCI may also gather further information about a service by, for example, sending out surveys, and they will then compile a summary that will help them decide whether there may be risks to people using the service.

If so, they could decide to bring forward a key inspection or carry out a random inspection.

What if a service doesn't measure up?

In most cases the CSCI is able to work cooperatively with services to ensure that necessary improvements are identified and carried out without the need for formal action.

Services they judge to be 'adequate' or 'poor' will be asked to submit an improvement plan explaining how they will develop their service and meet the requirements made.

Opportunity for feedback

At the conclusion of the inspection a small questionnaire will be left with care providers, asking for their comments as to how the inspection was conducted.

This is an important part of the inspection process since it provides the CSCI with helpful feedback, enabling them to identify areas where inspection practice needs to be improved and where they are getting things right.

HOW THE STANDARDS ARE USED

In assessing whether a care home or domiciliary care agency conforms to relevant regulations which are mandatory, the CSCI must take the care standards into account. However, the Commission may also take into account any other factors it considers relevant or reasonable to do so. Therefore compliance with the National Minimum Standards is not in itself enforceable, but compliance with regulations is, subject to the minimum standards being considered.

The regulators will look for evidence that the standards are being met and a good quality of life is being enjoyed by those individuals residing in care homes. It does so through discussions with the consumers of the service, their family and friends, and with the staff and managers of establishments, in addition to observations made of the day-to-day life within the home combined with scrutiny of policy.

The National Minimum Standards for Care Homes focus on realistic and achievable outcomes for consumers of services, ensuring that the minimum standard of facilities and provision of care service is reached within each establishment.

Standards for care homes

The standards for *care homes* are separated into topics and are based on issues that were deemed important by consumers actively receiving care home services and their families. The topics covered are:

- Choice of home (*Standards 1–6*)
- Health and personal care (*Standards 7–11*)
- Daily life and social activities (*Standards 12–15*)
- Complaints and protection (*Standards 16–18*)
- Environment (*Standards 19–26*)
- Staffing (*Standards 27–30*)
- Management and administration (*Standards 31–38*).

Standards for domicilary care agencies

The standards for *domiciliary care agencies* are separated into topics and are based on issues that were deemed important by consumers actively receiving care at home services and their families. The topics covered are:

- User-focused services (*Standards 1–6*)
- Personal care (*Standards 7–10*)
- Protection (*Standards 11–16*)
- Managers and staff (*Standards 17–21*)
- Organisation and running of the business (*Standards 22–27*).

Non-compliance

If you are unsure whether a care home or domiciliary care agency is complying with the standards, you can:

- Ask them directly who is responsible for the part you feel is not being adhered to.

- Contact the CSCI in any one of the ways suggested in Chapter 1 on finding services.

- If you have a social worker, ask them to deal with it.

By their very nature, the standards are 'open to interpretation' and may at any time be amended. Inspectors are also given a certain degree of 'discretion' when considering compliance.

For those of you with an interest, you can access the full set of standards by visiting the commission's website on http://www.csci.gov.uk. You may feel this to be appropriate if you have any concerns about a service provider meeting a standard, and you wish to see the relevant standard in its entirety before deciding on a course of action.

You will be aware from the discussion in earlier chapters, some of the standards are not applicable to employment agencies and I make clear which standards (or parts of standards where relevant) do not apply to agencies 'solely introducing workers'.

REMEMBER

The standards are the minimum below which care providers
must not allow their services to fall.

Part 2

Know the
Minimum Standards

12

Overview of the National Minimum Care Standards for Care Homes

NB: Adult placement schemes/homes for adults 18–65 have additional standards to which providers must adhere. For access to these visit www.csci.org.uk or call your local CSCI office for further information.

REMEMBER
The standards are the minimum below which a care provider must not allow their services to fall.

Change of term of reference
The consumer from this point forward will be referred to as the 'service user' as this is the official term used within the standards. Where I make comments and if appropriate for clarity I will still use the term 'consumer'.

CHOICE OF HOME (STANDARDS 1–6)

Standard 1 – Information

■ Each care home must produce a statement of purpose and a 'service users' guide' which sets out the aims and objectives, range of facilities and services it offers and its terms and conditions of occupancy. Copies of the most recent inspection report should also be made available.

- If a home claims within its information to be able to provide care for people with particular illnesses, e.g. dementia, then they will need to demonstrate how they will cater for those individuals.

- Where a service user is offered a care home place, and English is not their first language or whose culture dictates a certain diet, then a home will need to demonstrate they can provide for that consumer's needs, including making sure care staff are available who are able to communicate in the individual's mother tongue.

- Homes must make clear in their information whether they offer a friendly family-run or hotel-style environment and any other range of situations in between the two.

- The information should also include:
  - a description of the individual accommodation and communal space provided
  - relevant qualifications and experience of the registered provider, manager and staff
  - the number of places provided and any special needs or interests catered for
  - a copy of the complaints procedure
  - the views of consumers already 'resident' in the home.

- The information should be given in writing and in a relevant language/format detailing how to contact the office of the local CSCI, Social Services and healthcare authorities.

- The information should be given to potential consumers, but only if they request it. My advice is that you should insist on it, as there is no obligation on a care home's part to offer it. Remember, there is little value in learning the terms of a home *after* the service is being provided.

Standard 2 – Contract

- If care is paid for privately then expect to receive a written contract.

- If being funded by the local authority then they will already have a group contract with the care home, but service users should still expect to receive a statement of residency.

- **Key points that should be included in a contract**:
  - rooms to be occupied
  - overall care and services (including food) covered by fee
  - fees payable and by whom (service user, local authority, relative or other)
  - additional services to be paid for over and above those included in the fees
  - rights and obligations of the consumer of the service and those of the registered provider
  - who is liable if there is a breach of contract
  - terms of occupancy, including notice period
  - insurance.

Standard 3 – Needs Assessment

- When a home is chosen then the individual will need to be assessed by the home.

- If the council is paying for the care or you have already been involved with a professional in setting up the care, you may have had an assessment of needs carried out by the relevant professional, e.g. a social worker.

- It is common practice for professionals to share information with the care home, but some care homes may prefer to undertake their own assessment regardless.

- Assessments should be comprehensive, so if any previous assessment undertaken appears not to be as thorough, then you must ensure (for your own benefit) that gaps are filled in for the care home *prior* to admission.

- If you are paying for care independently, or there has been no previous involvement with health care professionals, then the registered person within the home must carry out an assessment of needs and this must cover:
  - personal care and physical well-being
  - diet and weight and dietary preferences
  - sight, hearing and communication
  - oral health
  - foot care
  - mobility and dexterity
  - history of falls
  - continence
  - medical usage
  - mental state and cognition
  - social interests, hobbies, religious and cultural needs
  - personal safety and risk
  - care and family involvement and other social contacts/ relationships.

- As an outcome of gaining this information, the care home must then devise a plan of care for daily living which can then be read by nursing and care workers to provide them with insight as to a service user's physical care requirements and preferences.

Standard 4 – Meeting Needs

- If a home claims to cater for a particular need, it must meet that need.

Standard 5 – Trial Visits

- Service users must be allowed (*irrespective of who is paying for the care*) to visit the home either alone, with friends, relatives or the even milkman if they choose! They must be given the opportunity to assess the quality of the facilities and the suitability of the home.

- Homes should invite service users to undertake a trial visit.

- If a service user is unable to visit the home, then a staff member from the care home should offer to visit at a location that suits the service user, e.g. at home or in hospital.

- Unfortunately not all care home admissions are foreseeable. In the event that a person has been admitted to a care home as an emergency (perhaps due to a sudden decline in health not warranting hospitalisation but putting them at risk if alone at home), then this should not mean that they receive less information. Service users should expect to have all of the information pertaining to the service user's guide within 48 hours of admission and all other admission criteria should be carried out within a maximum of five working days. If a service user is not in agreement with the conditions of the home they still have the same rights with regard to choice and can actively pursue an alternative care facility.

Standard 6 – Intermediate Care

■ Intermediate care is short-term care and the standards are clear as to its purpose. This is that any home claiming to provide such care must be focused on helping the service user maximise independence and return home at the earliest opportunity.

■ The home must have the resources, the equipment and the staffing available if offering the promotion of rehabilitation.

HEALTH AND PERSONAL CARE (STANDARDS 7–11)

Standard 7 – Service User Plan

■ The service user plan is devised from the information gathered during the assessment process and should be available for access by nurses/care workers and any other relevant healthcare professional, and it should pay particular attention to the prevention of falls.

■ The information should include a service user's physical, medical and social needs and must be reviewed by care staff at least once a month and updated to reflect changing needs and current objectives.

IN MY OPINION

I feel that the standards could have made provision that, in the event of a consumer having a high level of medical need and they are using a nursing home service, then such a review should be carried out by a qualified nurse. After all, some consumers buy into nursing home care service for the reassurance of the qualified personnel available to oversee their medical condition. Therefore don't be afraid to ask that a review be carried out by a qualified individual if it is felt to be necessary to a consumer's care. Any good care home provider would understand and respond to any anxiety felt.

■ Such drawing up of the plan and any subsequent changes must be done with the service user's full involvement or that of a representative of their choice, and agreed and signed by the service user or their representative.

Standard 8 – Health Care

■ This standard aims to ensure that the service user's healthcare needs are fully met and therefore the care home staff should ensure the following:

– They meet the assessed needs.

– Oral hygiene is maintained at a level acceptable to the service user.

– Where applicable, service users are assessed by a person trained to assess the risk of developing pressure sores and an action plan developed to reduce the risk and treat the condition if necessary. In the event of pressure-sore care being required, the home must ensure relevant equipment is available.

– The service user's psychological health is monitored regularly.

– Opportunities must be available to service users for appropriate exercise and physical activities while being realistic as to their limitations.

– Service users are weighed on a regular basis and their nutritional health monitored. Records must be kept.

IN MY VIEW – BEST PRACTICE

If a consumer enters a care home, they should expect to be weighed and re-weighed on a regular basis. But what is a regular basis?

I don't think that weekly weighing would be unreasonable, but at the very least I think that weight should be monitored monthly. By having regular weighings, a home will be able to monitor whether a consumer's weight is in decline and act on such weight loss quickly, before a consumer suffers a condition such as mal-nutrition.

Any good care home would enlist the help of a nutritionist at the first sign of a decline in weight, having of course first sought advice to eliminate any medical reason for the loss.

There are many approaches one can take to keep health and weight at an opti-mum levels including food supplements for those who are off their food for whatever reason.

However, care homes should also be vigilant as to the consumer's eating habits and if an individual is not eating regularly, time must be taken to discuss this with the person directly or, where necessary, with other professionals.

Maybe a consumer is upset about something or just does not like the food, its presentation or the time or the manner in which it is served.

It does happen that some older people have a small appetite, but it is not a for-gone conclusion and such a loss should never be shrugged off and blamed on old age, a fussy child, etc. It should be investigated for the cause and a plan of action generated to make the management of the problem clear.

- Service users should be allowed to:
  - register with a GP of choice (if the GP is in agreement)

- have access to specialist medical, nursing, dental, pharma-
  ceutical, chiropody and therapeutic services and care from
  hospitals and community health services
- have access to hearing and sight tests
- have their right to NHS services upheld.

Standard 9 – Medication

■ If a service user takes medication, there are two issues to
consider:

- Are they able to administer their own medication?
- If so, would they want to self-administer?

■ If service users are able to take responsibility for their own
medication, and if they wish to do so, then any potential risks
associated with self-administration must be identified. If,
following assessment, it is decided that self-administration is
appropriate, the home must provide individuals with a
lockable space in which to store medication. Only trained
and designated care staff may have access to it with the
permission of the service user.

■ The care home must have a medication policy and ensure staff
adherence to it at all times. Policy must cover procedures for
the receipt, recording, storage, handling, administration and
disposal of medicines.

■ Records must be kept of all medicines received, administered
and leaving the home or disposed of to ensure that there is no
mishandling. Records of current medication for each service
user (including those self-administering) must be kept.

■ Controlled drugs administered by staff must be stored in a
metal cupboard, and, for those receiving nursing care,

administered by a medical practitioner or registered nurse only.

■ In residential care homes, all medicines, including controlled drugs (except those for self-administration), should be administered by designated and appropriately-trained staff and the administration of controlled drugs must be witnessed by another designated, appropriately-trained member of staff.

■ Any training of care staff in respect of medication must be accredited.

■ Staff must monitor the condition of individuals who are receiving medication and call in a GP if they are concerned about any change in condition that may be a result of medication.

■ Reviews of medication should be carried out on a regular basis.

Standard 10 – Privacy and Dignity

■ The arrangements for health and personal care within the care home should ensure that the privacy and dignity of the service users are respected at all times.

■ Care staff should be particularly sensitive and mindful of the right to dignity when involved in personal care-giving of the of the service user including:
  – nursing
  – bathing
  – washing (and if a service user has chosen to share a room, screening is provided to ensure privacy is not compromised when personal care is being given or at any other time)

- – using the toilet or commode.

■ Service users have an absolute right to privacy at times such as:
  - – during a consultation with or an examination by health and social care professionals (medical examinations and treatment must be provided in your own room)
  - – consultation with legal and financial advisers
  - – in maintaining social contacts with relatives and friends
  - – staff entering bedrooms, toilets and bathrooms (they should always knock on the door and wait to be called in).

■ Service users should have easy access to a telephone for private use and should always receive mail unopened.

■ Staff must call service users by the name they prefer and use that at all times.

■ All staff must be trained during induction on how to treat service users with respect at all times.

Standard 11 – Dying and Death

■ The standards state that care and comfort are given to service users who are dying and their death must be handled with dignity and propriety while their spiritual needs, rites and functions are observed.

THINK ABOUT THIS

Unless issues such as a person's spiritual beliefs are discussed with a home, simply being told that someone is a Christian will not provide adequate information for the home to know exactly how they would like their death to be celebrated. So consideration must be given to this matter and discussions held with the care home regarding any strong views on how an individual (and where applicable their family) would like to be dealt with at this very sensitive time.

> As hard as it may be, I strongly suggest that all potential care home users who are in a position to do so discuss their wishes with friends/family or advocates prior to admission, and that the decision be extended to the care home in order that such wishes will be respected upon death.

■ Care staff must make every effort to ensure that those who are terminally ill receive appropriate attention and pain relief throughout their final days, and wishes concerning terminal care and arrangements after death should be discussed with individuals and carried out when the time arises.

■ Service users must be able to spend their final days in their own room, surrounded by their personal belongings, unless there are strong medical reasons to prevent this.

■ The home must also ensure that if any staff member or other service user wishes to offer comfort to the person who is dying, then they are enabled and supported to do so.

■ If the terminally ill person wishes to receive palliative care, practical assistance and advice or bereavement counselling (one assumes for the family of the dying person) provided by trained professionals/specialist agencies, it must be made available.

> **IN MY VIEW**
> Good care homes will also make sure counselling services are accessible to workers or other consumers of the care service. The standards do not make clear whether a home could charge for such bereavement counselling.

■ Relatives and friends of an individual who is dying must be allowed to stay with him/her for as long as they wish, unless the individual makes it clear that he or she does not want them there.

▪ A person who has died must be handled with dignity, and time allowed for family and friends to pay their respects.

▪ Policies and procedures for handling dying and death must be in place and observed by staff.

▪ Family and friends should be involved (if that is what the dying individual wants) in planning for and dealing with increasing infirmity, terminal illness and death.

▪ Planning could take many forms and may include decisions on pain relief and, if appropriate, discussion on whether to continue treatment.

AS DIFFICULT AS IT MIGHT BE

Decisions about death, if left solely to friends or family members, can inevitably be difficult and upsetting and will come at a time when they may already be finding the situation hard to cope with.

This raises the question of whether the time of one's imminent death is the best time to be making such decisions.

The more information a care home is provided with prior to a consumer facing death, the easier the situation will be for those left behind.

DAILY LIFE AND SOCIAL ACTIVITIES (STANDARDS 12–15)

Standard 12 – Social Contact and Activities

■ Any routines of daily living and activities made available must be flexible and varied to suit all service users' expectations, preferences and capacities.

■ Service users must have the opportunity to exercise choice in relation to:
  – leisure and social activities and cultural interests
  – food, meals and mealtimes
  – routines of daily living
  – personal and social relationships
  – religious observance.

■ Interests should be recorded and service users must be given opportunities for stimulation through leisure and recreational activities in and outside the home.

■ Up-to-date information about activities must be circulated to all service users in formats suited to their capacities.

Standard 13 – Community Contact

■ The community contact standard is aimed at maintaining contact with family/friends/representatives and the local community.

■ Service users should:
  – be able to have visitors at any reasonable time and links with the local community should be developed and/or maintained in accordance with their preferences

- be allowed to receive visitors in private and be able to choose whom they see and do not see
- not have restrictions imposed upon them in relation to who can visit *except* when requested to do so by the service user, and their wishes must be recorded
- at the time of moving into the home, be given written information about the home's policy on maintaining the involvement of relatives and friends, as should all interested individuals including the representatives of a service user.

■ Involvement in the home by local community groups and/or volunteers should accord with the preferences of each service user.

Standard 14 – Autonomy and Choice

■ Service users should be helped to exercise choice and control over their life.

■ The home must maximise a service user's opportunities to exercise personal autonomy and choice such as allowing them to handle their own financial affairs for as long as they wish to and have the capacity to do so.

■ Service users, their relatives and friends must be informed of how to contact external agents (e.g. advocates) who will act in their interests.

■ Service users are entitled to bring personal possessions with them, the extent of which should be agreed prior to admission.

■ Finally, access to personal records, in accordance with the Data

Protection Act 1998, must be assisted if a service user wishes to access them.

Standard 15 – Meals and Mealtimes

■ The home must ensure that service users receive a varied, appealing, wholesome and nutritious diet, which is suited to individually assessed and recorded requirements, and that meals are taken in a congenial setting and at flexible times.

■ Three full meals must be offered each day (at least one of which must be cooked) at intervals of not more than five hours.

■ Hot and cold drinks and snacks should be available at all times and offered regularly. A snack meal should be offered in the evening. The time lapse between the evening snack and breakfast the following morning should be no more than 12 hours.

■ Food, including liquified meals, should be presented in a manner which is attractive and appealing in terms of texture, flavour, and appearance, in order to maintain appetite and nutrition.

■ Special diets and religious or cultural dietary needs should be catered for as agreed at admission and recorded in the care plan.

■ Food for special occasions must be available.

■ There should be a menu (changed regularly) offering a choice of meals in written or other formats to suit the capacities of all service users. This must be given, read or explained to individuals using the service. 'Regularly' is open to interpretation, but I expect homes to change their menu at least every couple of months, if not more regularly.

- Mealtimes must be unhurried and allow sufficient time for service users to eat.

- Workers should be ready to offer assistance in eating where necessary, discreetly, sensitively and individually, while independent eating should be encouraged for as long as possible.

COMPLAINTS AND PROTECTION (STANDARDS 16–18)

Standard 16 – Complaints

- Service users, their relatives and friends should be confident that any complaints they have will be listened to, taken seriously and acted upon.

- The home must have a simple, clear and accessible complaints procedure which includes the stages and timescales for the process, showing that complaints are dealt with promptly and effectively. It should also show how to complain, and to whom, and have an assurance that 28 days will be the maximum time lapse before a response is received.

- Records should be kept of all complaints, and must include details of investigations and any action taken.

- Service users or anyone on their behalf are free to refer complaints at any time to the CSCI and should receive written information from the home on how to do so.

Standard 17 – Rights

■ Service users' legal rights must be protected and they must be free to exercise them at any time.

■ Where an individual lacks capacity, then the home must assist access to available advocacy services on the person's behalf.

■ The individual's right to participate in the political process must also be upheld, for example by enabling service users to vote in elections.

Standard 18 – Protection

■ Service users must be safeguarded from physical, financial, material, psychological or sexual abuse, neglect, discriminatory abuse or self-harm, and inhuman or degrading treatment, whether through deliberate intent, negligence or ignorance.

■ Robust procedures for responding to suspicion or evidence of abuse or neglect must ensure safety and protection, including passing on concerns to the CSCI.

■ All allegations and incidents of abuse must be followed up promptly and any action taken must be recorded.

■ The policies and practices of the home must ensure that any physical and/or verbal aggression by users of its service is understood and dealt with appropriately, and that physical intervention is used only as a last resort.

■ The home's policies and practices regarding money and financial affairs must ensure that access to a service user's personal financial records is always appropriate, and that there are systems of safe storage of money and valuables, that consultation on finances are always in private, and advice on personal insurance is given if required.

■ Staff involvement in assisting in the making of or benefiting from a service user's will must be strictly prohibited.

ENVIRONMENT (STANDARDS 19–26)

Standard 19 – Premises

■ The location and layout of the home must be suitable for its stated purpose and:
 – be accessible
 – be safe and well-maintained
 – meet service users' individual and collective needs in a comfortable and homely way
 – have been designed with reference to relevant guidance.

■ A programme of routine maintenance and renewal of the fabric and decoration of the premises must be produced and carried out with records kept.

■ The care home grounds should be kept tidy, safe, attractive and accessible to all users of its service, and allow access to sunlight.

■ The building must comply with the requirements of the local fire service and environmental health department.

■ The use of CCTV cameras is restricted to entrance areas for security purposes only and must not intrude on service users' daily lives.

Standard 20 – Shared Facilities

■ For comfort and happiness service users must have access to safe and comfortable indoor, outdoor and communal facilities.

■ Communal space should be available which includes rooms in which a variety of social, cultural and religious activities can take place and service users can meet visitors in private.

■ Dining room(s) must cater for all service users and if smoking is permitted then there must be a dedicated room for smoking.

■ There should be outdoor space with seating and it must be accessible to those in wheelchairs or with other mobility problems. The design of the outdoor space must meet the needs of all service users including those with physical, sensory or cognitive impairments.

■ Lighting in communal rooms must be domestic in character. Lighting must be sufficiently bright and positioned to enable individuals to read or undertake other activities.

■ Furnishings of communal rooms must be domestic in character and of good quality, and suitable for the range of interests and activities of the service users.

Standard 21 – Lavatories and Washing Facilities

■ Care homes must have sufficient and suitable lavatories and washing and bathing facilities to meet the needs of all the users of the service.

■ There must be accessible toilets, clearly marked, and for convenience these must be close to lounge and dining areas, and there must be a toilet within close proximity of each service user's private accommodation.

- All homes must have a ratio of one assisted bath (or assisted shower provided this meets residents' needs) to eight consumers.

- En-suite facilities (at minimum a toilet and hand-basin) must be provided to all service users in all new-builds, extensions and all first-time registrations from 1 April 2002.

- The installation of en-suite facilities should be in addition to the minimum usable floor space standards.

- En-suite facilities in rooms accommodating individuals using wheelchairs or other aids must be accessible to them.

- Sluice facilities must be provided separately from WC and bathing facilities.

Standard 22 – Adaptations and Equipment

- Care homes have a responsibility to ensure that any user of their services has the specialist equipment they require to maximise their independence.

- The home must demonstrate that an assessment of the premises and facilities has been made by suitably qualified persons, including a qualified occupational therapist, with specialist knowledge of the client groups catered for.

- Evidence must be produced showing that any recommended disability equipment has been secured or provided and that environmental adaptations are made to meet the needs of varied individuals.

- Service users should have access to all parts of the communal and private space, through the provision of ramps and passenger lifts where required to achieve this, or stair/chair lifts where they meet the assessed needs of individuals.

- The home must provide grab rails and other aids in corridors, bathrooms, toilets, communal rooms and where necessary in a service user's accommodation.

- Aids, hoists and assisted toilets and baths must be installed which are capable of meeting the assessed needs of all those using the service.

- Doorways into communal areas, individual rooms, bathing and toilet facilities and other spaces to which wheelchair users must have access should be of sufficient width to permit access.

- Facilities, including communication aids (e.g. a loop system), and signs must be provided where necessary taking account of the needs of individuals and taking account of the needs, for example, of those with hearing impairment, visual impairment, dual sensory impairments, learning disabilities or dementia or other cognitive impairment.

- Storage areas must be provided for aids and equipment, including wheelchairs.

- Call systems with an accessible alarm facility must also be provided in every room.

Standard 23 – Individual Accommodation – Space Requirements

■ A service user's bedroom must suit their needs.

■ Room dimensions and layout options must ensure that there is room on either side of the bed to enable access for care staff and any equipment if needed.

■ Where rooms are shared (*some people choose this option as it can reduce the fees*), they must not be occupied by more than two service users who have made a positive choice to share with each other.

■ Screening should be provided in double rooms to ensure privacy for personal care.

■ If an individual is in a shared room and the other place becomes vacant, they should be given the opportunity to choose not to share, by moving into a different room if necessary.

■ Rooms which are currently shared must have at least 16 square metres of usable floor space (excluding en-suite facilities) and any new-build with shared bedrooms must also provide the sharers with a second room, such as a sitting room.

Standard 24 – Furniture and Fittings

■ Service users must live in a safe and comfortable environment and their bedroom should enable them to have some of their own possessions around them.

■ The home must provide service users with private accommodation which is furnished and equipped to assure comfort and privacy and meet assessed needs.

■ Should service users choose not to bring their own furnishings, then individual bedrooms must be provided with, as a minimum:
  - a clean comfortable bed, minimum 900 mm wide, at a suitable, safe height for the consumer
  - bed-linen
  - curtains or blinds
  - mirror
  - overhead and bedside lighting
  - comfortable seating for two people
  - drawers and enclosed space for hanging clothes
  - at least two accessible double electric sockets
  - a table to sit at and a bedside table
  - handbasin (unless en-suite provided).

■ Any recipient of nursing care must be provided with an adjustable bed.

■ Bedrooms should be carpeted or have a suitable alternative floor-covering.

■ The door to private accommodation should be fitted with locks suited to the service user's capabilities and accessible to staff in emergencies.

■ Keys to a service user's room must be provided unless a risk assessment suggests that individuals should not have one.

■ A lockable storage space for medication, money and valuables should also be provided (unless the reason for not doing so is explained in the care plan).

Standard 25 – Heating and Lighting

- The heating, lighting, water supply and ventilation of accommodation must meet the relevant environmental health and safety requirements and the needs of individual service users.

- Rooms should be individually and naturally ventilated and, if the establishment is newly built, the height of the window should enable service users to see out of it when seated or in bed.

- Rooms must be centrally heated and such heating must be able to be controlled in an individual's room.

- For obvious safety reasons, pipework and radiators must be guarded or have guaranteed low-temperature surfaces.

- Lighting in the service user's accommodation must be domestic in character and include table-level lamp lighting, and emergency lighting must be provided throughout the home.

Standard 26 – Hygiene and Control of Infection

- The care home must be kept clean, hygienic and free from offensive odours throughout and systems must be in place to control the spread of infection, in accordance with relevant legislation and published professional guidance.

- Service users and their visitors should not be subjected to watching care home workers transport dirty laundry through areas where food is stored, prepared, cooked or eaten, nor should staff carrying laundry intrude on an individual's personal environment.

- Policies and procedures for control of infection, including the safe handling and disposal of clinical waste, dealing with spillages, provision of protective clothing and hand washing, must be in place.

- Washing machines must have the specified programming ability to meet disinfection standards.

STAFFING (STANDARDS 27–30)

Standard 27 – Staff Complement

- Staffing numbers and the skill mix of qualified/unqualified workers must at all times be appropriate to the assessed needs of the service users and the size, layout and purpose of the home.

- A recorded staff rota must be kept showing which workers are on duty at any time during the day and night, and in what capacity.

- The ratios of care workers to service users must be determined according to the assessed needs of residents, and a system operated for calculating staff numbers required, in accordance with guidance recommended by the Department of Health.

I WOULD SUGGEST...

If you are in any way concerned that the home does not have adequate staffing, ask them how they have determined the number of staff they require. If they do not say it is based on the Department of Health recommended guidance, you should refer your concerns to the CSCI for further investigation.

- Additional staff must be on duty at peak times of activity during the day.

- There must be waking night workers on duty in numbers that reflect the numbers and needs of the service users and the layout of the home. In care homes providing nursing, this includes registered nurse(s).

- Workers providing personal care must be aged at least 18 years and workers left in charge of the home should be aged at least 21 years.

- Domestic staff must be employed in sufficient numbers to ensure that standards relating to food, meals and nutrition are fully met, and that the home is maintained in a clean and hygienic state, free from dirt and unpleasant odours.

Standard 28 – Qualifications

- The standards state that trainees (including all workers under 18) are registered on a certified training programme and a minimum of 50 per cent of care staff must be trained at National Vocational Qualification Level 2 in care or equivalent.

- The ratio excludes the registered manager and/or care manager, and in care homes providing nursing, excludes those members of the care staff who are registered nurses. Any agency staff working in the home will be included in the 50 per cent ratio.

Standard 29 – Recruitment

- The home must operate a thorough recruitment procedure based on equal opportunities and ensuring the protection of users of the service.

■ Two written references must be obtained before appointing a member of staff, and any gaps in employment records must be explored.

■ New workers must only be confirmed in their post following completion of a Criminal Records Bureau (CRB) check which includes a police check, satisfactory check of the Protection of Children Act, Vulnerable Adults (POCA/POVA) lists, and, if applicable, a separate check of qualified nurses on the NMC register.

■ Workers must be employed in accordance with the code of conduct and practice set by the GSCC and given copies of the code.

■ All workers must receive statements of terms and conditions of employment.

■ The recruitment and selection process for any volunteers involved in the home must still be thorough and include CRB checks.

Standard 30 – Staff Training

■ The home must ensure that there are staff training and development programmes which meet the National Training Organisation (NTO) workforce training targets and ensure workers fulfil the aims of the home and meet the changing needs of service users.

■ All members of staff must receive induction training to NTO specification within six weeks of appointment to their posts, including training on the principles of care, safe working practices, the organisation and worker role, the experiences and particular needs of the user group, and the influences and particular requirements of the service setting.

- All workers must receive foundation training to NTO specification within the first six months of appointment which equips them to meet the assessed needs of the service users accommodated, as defined in their individual plan of care.

- All workers must receive a minimum of three paid days' training per year (including in-house training), and have an individual training and development assessment and profile.

MANAGEMENT AND ADMINISTRATION (STANDARDS 31–38)

Standard 31 – Day-to-Day Operations

- The registered manager must be qualified, competent and experienced to run the home and meet its stated purpose, aims and objectives.

- The registered manager must have at least two years' experience in a senior management capacity in the managing of a relevant care setting within the past five years and a qualification, at Level 4 NVQ, in management and care or equivalent.

- When nursing care is provided by the home (e.g. by a nursing home), the manager must be a first-level registered nurse and hold a relevant management qualification.

- The registered manager must not be responsible for more than one registered establishment.

■ They must be able to demonstrate that they have undertaken periodic training to update their knowledge, skills and competence while managing the home.

■ The manager and other senior workers must be familiar with the conditions/diseases associated with old age.

■ The job description of the registered manager must enable him/her to take responsibility for fulfilling his/her duties.

■ There must be clear lines of accountability within the home and with any external management.

Standard 32 – Ethos

■ The registered manager must ensure that the management approach of the home creates an open, positive and inclusive atmosphere and communicates a clear sense of direction and leadership which workers and users of the service understand and relate to.

■ The registered manager must have strategies for enabling workers, service users and other stakeholders to affect the way in which the service is delivered.

■ The processes of managing and running the home must be open and transparent, and planning and practice must encourage innovation, creativity and development.

■ A commitment must be made to equal opportunities within organisations.

Standard 33 – Quality Assurance

■ Effective quality assurance and quality monitoring systems are based on seeking the views of service users. Homes must therefore ensure such monitoring systems are in place to measure success in meeting the aims, objectives and statement of purpose of the home.

■ There must be an annual development plan for the home, based on a systematic cycle of planning – action – review, reflecting the aims and outcomes for the service user. The results of surveys must be published and made available to current and prospective users, their representatives and other interested parties, including the CSCI.

■ The registered manager and workers must demonstrate a commitment to lifelong learning and development for each user of its service, linked to the implementation of his/her individual care plan.

■ Feedback should be actively sought from service users about services provided through different means such as anonymous user-satisfaction questionnaires and individual and group discussion, as well as evidence from records and life plans. This should inform all planning and reviews.

■ Family, friends and stakeholders within the community such as GPs, chiropodists and voluntary organisation staff should be approached by the home for their views and opinions on how the home is achieving goals for consumers.

> **YOU SHOULD ...**
> Ask to see a sample of such views and opinions when visiting homes.

■ Service users must be told about planned CSCI inspections and given access to inspectors, and the views of users of the service must be made available to CSCI inspectors for inclusion in inspection reports.

■ Service users do not have a right to be notified if there is to be an unannounced inspection.

Standard 34 – Financial Procedures

■ Suitable accounting and financial procedures must be adopted to demonstrate current financial viability and to ensure there is effective and efficient management of the business.

■ Insurance cover must be in place to safeguard against loss of or damage to the assets of the business. The level of cover should reflect the full replacement value of buildings, fixtures, fittings and equipment.

■ Insurance cover should be obtained for business interruption costs (including loss of earnings), as well as costs to the operator of meeting its contractual liabilities. The latter must be sufficient to cover the registered person's legal liabilities to employees, service users and third-party persons to a limit commensurate with the level and extent of activities undertaken or to a minimum of £5 million.

■ Records must be kept of all transactions entered into by the registered person and there must be a business and financial plan for the establishment, open to inspection and reviewed annually.

IN REALITY

There is no access for consumers to the financial records of care homes but the CSCI do have the power to access such records in the event that they have concerns for the financial stability of an establishment.

Standard 35 – Service User's Money

- Service users must have control of their own money, except where either they state that they do not wish to or they lack capacity.

- Safeguards must be in place to protect their financial interests if service users are not in control of their own money, and where this is applicable written records of all transactions must be kept.

- Where the money of more than one individual is handled, the manager must ensure that the personal allowances of those individuals are not pooled and appropriate records and receipts for transactions must be kept.

- **The registered manager may be appointed as agent for a service user only where no other individual is available. In this case, the manager ensures that:**
  - the registration authority is notified on inspection
  - records are kept of all incoming and outgoing payments.

- Secure facilities must be provided for the safe keeping of money and valuables on behalf of the service user and records and receipts must be kept of possessions handed over for safe keeping.

Standard 36 – Staff Supervision

- The home must ensure that its employment policies and procedures in relation to its induction, training and supervision arrangements are put into practice.

- Care workers must receive formal supervision at least six times a year. Supervision covers:

- all aspects of practice
- philosophy of care in the home
- career development needs.

■ Supervision means that a more experienced/qualified staff member will be monitoring the standard of care the worker is providing to the residents. It is a good opportunity for managers to discuss any areas of development required to improve the provision of care or to request feedback from service users/co-workers of the worker being supervised.

■ All other workers (such as domestic staff) must be supervised as part of the normal management process on a continuous basis.

■ Volunteers must also receive training, supervision and support appropriate to their role and must not be used to replace paid workers, but can be used in addition to them.

Standard 37 – Record-Keeping

■ Records required by regulation for the protection of service users and for the effective and efficient running of the business must be maintained, up to date and accurate.

■ Service users must have access to their records and information about them held by the home, as well as being given an opportunity to help maintain personal records.

> **HOW?**
> Ask potential homes how they may extend this right to you.

■ Individual records and home records must be secure, up to date and in good order and be constructed, maintained and used in accordance with the Data Protection Act 1998 and other statutory requirements.

Standard 38 – Safe Working Practices

■ The registered manager should ensure safe working practices including:

– **Moving and handling** – use of techniques for moving people and objects in order to avoid injury to recipients of care or workers.

– **Fire safety** – understanding and implementation of appropriate fire procedures.

– **First aid** – knowledge of how to deal with accidents and health emergencies; provision of a first aid box and a qualified first aider at all times; the recording of all cases.

– **Food hygiene** – correct storage and preparation of food to avoid food poisoning, including labelling and dating of stored food.

– **Infection control** – understanding and practice of measures to prevent spread of infection and communicable diseases.

■ The registered manager must also ensure the health and safety of service users and workers including:

– safe storage and disposal of hazardous substances

– regular servicing of boilers and central heating systems under contract by competent persons (e.g. members of the Council of Registered Gas Installers (CORGI))

– maintenance of electrical systems and electrical equipment

– regulation of water temperature, and design solutions to

control the risk of legionella and risks from hot water/ surfaces (e.g. temperature close to 43°C)

- provision and maintenance of window restrictors based on assessment of vulnerability and risk to consumers of the service
- maintenance of a safe environment including kitchen equipment and laundry machinery, outdoor steps and pathways, gardening equipment
- security of the premises
- security of individuals based on an assessment of vulnerability.

■ The registered manager must also ensure compliance with relevant legislation including:
   - a written statement of the policy regarding, organisation of and arrangements for maintaining safe working practices
   - risk assessments carried out for all safe working practice topics and any significant findings of the risk assessment recorded
   - all accidents, injuries and incidents of illness or communicable disease recorded and reported to relevant bodies
   - safety procedures displayed and explained in formats that are easily understood, and that take account of any special communication needs of the service user.

13

Overview of National Minimum Care Standards for Domiciliary Care Agencies

NB: Nursing agencies have additional standards to which providers must adhere. For access to these visit www.csci.org.uk or call your local CSCI office for further information.

> **REMEMBER**
> The standards are the minimum below which care providers
> must not allow their services to fall.

Change of term of reference
The consumer from this point forward will be referred to as the 'service user' as this is the official term used within the standards. Where I make comments and if appropriate for clarity I will still use the term 'consumer'.

USER-FOCUSED SERVICES (STANDARDS 1–6)

Standard 1 – Information

■ Each provider of a domiciliary care service must produce a Statement of Purpose and a Service Users' Guide for current and prospective service users and their relatives and it must contain up-to-date information on the organisation.

■ The Service Users' Guide should include:
  - the aims and objectives of the agency
  - the nature of the services provided, including specialist services
  - the people for whom the service is provided
  - an overview of the process for the delivery of care
  - support from initial referral, through needs and risk assessment
  - the development of the service user plan
  - review of the care and reassessment of need
  - key contract terms and conditions
  - the complaints procedure
  - the Quality Assurance process
  - specific information on key policies and procedures
  - how to contact the local offices of the Commission for Social Care Inspectorate, Social Services, healthcare authorities and the General Social Services Council (GSCC)
  - hours of operation
  - details of insurance cover.

■ The literature must be written in plain English and made available in appropriate formats, e.g. large print, Braille.

- Where services are or may be provided to people for whom English is not their first language, documents must also be made available in the language of their choice.

Standard 2 – Care Needs Assessment

- Service users should expect an assessment by the care provider prior to the provision of a domiciliary care service (or within two working days in exceptional circumstances), and this should be carried out by people who are trained to do so, using appropriate methods of communication so that service users and/or their representatives are fully involved.

A POINT TO CONSIDER

Some consumers may find the idea of assessment intrusive and feel that the fewer visits the better. However, the assessment stage is a good time to decide if a care organisation is likeable. It is not always easy to assess this purely from literature and regardless of who is paying for care, consumers should ask for a home assessment if they would not find such a second assessment a burden in order that they can themselves assess the care provider.

- If care is being funded by social services, local authority or health trust, then the standards do appear to allow for providers to obtain a summary of health needs. But inspectors are given discretionary powers and the widespread view is that providers should obtain their own assessment of needs. Prudent ones will – especially if they employ their workers because they have a duty to comply with health and safety legislation. They should assess the environment in which employees work. My advice would be to use only organisations who undertake their own assessments.

■ Assessments should cover:
  - the type of personal care that a service user requires for their physical well-being
  - any involvement from family or friends
  - their level of sight, hearing and communication
  - issues of continence
  - their physical condition in terms of mobility, dexterity and the need for disability equipment
  - whether they have any problems with their mental health and cognition
  - their medication requirements
  - all aspects of personal safety and risk both for the service user and any potential care worker visiting the home
  - any specific condition-related needs and specialist input required
  - dietary requirements and preferences (if the care worker is to be involved in this aspect of daily living)
  - social interests
  - religious and cultural needs (if deemed appropriate for workers to know them)
  - the preferred method of communication
  - the method of payment for the service.

■ This information should then be written into a usable document and agreed by the service user. Once agreement is reached, the care or support worker must be provided with a copy so that they are aware of any special needs and the activities that they are required to undertake.

■ In the event of a service user requiring care at short notice or in a crisis, and a care needs assessment hasn't been undertaken prior to care delivery, then the person providing the direct care must be trained and able to undertake an initial contact assessment during the first visit if required.

■ Procedures must be in place so that care and support workers can recognise and report changes in care needs or circumstances, in order that a reassessment can be arranged.

■ Regular reassessments must be undertaken by the agency at least once a year.

Standard 3 – Meeting Needs

■ The organisation must collectively have the skills and experience to deliver the services and care which the agency states in its information material that it can provide and the skills and experience of care workers must then be matched to the care needs.

■ Care workers must be able to communicate effectively with service users via the service user's preferred method of communication, e.g. sign language, computer, etc.

■ Any specialised services offered (and identified in the Service Users' Guide) must be based on current good practice, be relevant to the agency and reflect relevant specialist and clinical guidance. If services are therefore offered to people with dementia, mental health problems, sensory impairment, physical disabilities, learning disabilities, substance misuse problems, intermediate or respite care, then the agency must demonstrate that it can provide a good level of service to anyone with such a condition.

■ When services are provided for specific minority ethnic communities or social/cultural or religious groups, their particular requirements and preferences must be identified, understood and entered into the care plan.

Standard 4 – Contract (except for employment agencies solely introducing workers)

■ The agency must issue a written contract (if self-funding) within seven days of commencement of the service.

■ The contract between the service user and the provider must specify the following, (unless these appear in the Service Users' Guide and care plan):

- the name, address and telephone number of the agency
- a contact number for out of hours and details of how to access the service
- a contact number for the office of regular care workers and their manager
- any areas of activity which home care or support workers will and will not undertake and the degree of flexibility in the provision of personal care
- the circumstances in which the service may be cancelled or withdrawn including temporary cancellation by the service user
- the fees payable for the service, and by whom
- the rights and responsibilities of both parties (including insurance) and liability if there is a breach of contract or any damage occurring in the home
- any arrangements for monitoring and reviewing of a service user's needs and for updating the assessment and the individual care plan
- the process for assuring the quality of the service,

> monitoring and supervision of workers

- – supplies and/or equipment to be made available by service users and by the agency
- – the respective responsibilities of the agency and the service user in relation to health and safety matters
- – the arrangements to cover holidays and sickness
- – key-holding and other arrangements agreed for entering or leaving the home.

■ The service user and/or their relatives or representative and the agency must each have a signed copy of the contract which is signed by the service user (or their named representative) and the registered manager on behalf of the organisation.

REMEMBER

You must have an opportunity to peruse the contract prior to accepting a service as there is no value to finding out that you do not agree with key terms *after a* service is being provided.

Standard 5 – Confidentiality

■ Care and support workers must respect information given by the service user or their representatives in confidence and handle that information in accordance with the Data Protection Act 1998 and the agency's written policies and procedures, and they must always do so in the best interests of the service user.

■ Service users should receive summaries of the agency's policies and procedures on confidentiality which specify the circumstances under which confidentiality may be breached and includes the process for dealing with inappropriate breaches (*except for employment agencies solely introducing workers*).

■ Care or support workers need to know when information given them in confidence must be shared with their manager and other social/healthcare agencies (*except for employment agencies solely introducing workers*).

■ The principles of confidentiality must be observed in discussion with colleagues and the line manager, particularly when undertaking training or group supervision sessions.

■ Suitable provision must be made for the safe and confidential storage of service user records within the agency offices, to include the provision of lockable filing cabinets and the shielding of computer screens from general view when displaying personal data.

Standard 6 – Responsive Services

■ Workers provided by the agency must be reliable and dependable and able to respond flexibly to needs which arise on a day-to-day basis, and services should be provided in a way that meets the outcomes identified in the care plan.

■ Workers should arrive at the home within the time band specified and work for the full amount of time allocated. Upon arrival they should ask the service user if there are any particular personal care needs or requirements they have on that visit (*except for employment agencies solely introducing workers*).

■ There should be continuity in relation to the care or support worker(s) who are providing care and they should be changed

only for legitimate reasons, for example:
- they are sick
- on holiday
- undertaking training
- have left the organisation
- if the service requirements change and the care worker does not have the necessary skills, physical capacity or specialist training
- the care or support worker is unavailable for additional hours or changed times
- if the service user's request for change is for legitimate reasons
- if a non-professional relationship has developed between the service user and the worker
- to provide relief for care or support for those working in stressful environments
- to protect the care or support worker from abuse or discrimination (*except for employment agencies solely introducing workers*).

■ Service users or their relatives or representatives should be consulted in advance whenever possible and involved in the decision about the change of care or support worker if the change is permanent or likely to last longer than 30 days.

■ Service users should at all times be kept fully informed on issues relating to their care and, with the service user's consent, their relatives and/or representatives should also be kept informed.

PERSONAL CARE (STANDARDS 7–10)

Standard 7 – Service User Plan (except for employment agencies solely introducing workers)

■ A personal service user plan outlining arrangements for their care must be developed and agreed with them and should provide the basis on which the care will be delivered.

■ The plan should be generated from the care needs assessment, risk and manual handling risk assessment and the service contract or statement of terms and conditions, and set out in detail the action that will be taken by care and support workers to meet assessed needs. This includes specialist and communication requirements and identifies the areas of flexibility to enable service users to maximise their potential and maintain their independence. It should be drawn up with the service user's involvement whenever possible or with their representative, relatives or friends and/or any other professional felt appropriate to deal with this on the service user's behalf. It must take into account the service user's wishes and preferences in relation to the way in which the care is provided and their own chosen lifestyle – as long as it conforms to legal requirements and does not compromise the provider agency's obligations in law.

■ The plan should establish individualised procedures in relation to the taking of risks in daily living.

■ For individuals who are likely to be aggressive, abusive or cause harm or self-harm, it must focus on positive behaviour.

■ The information and detail provided in the plan must be appropriate for the complexity of the service to be provided and must be reviewed as changes in circumstances require it but at least *annually*, and reviewed with the service user, their relatives, friends and significant professionals.

■ Service users can also request a review as can a representative on their behalf if there has been a change in care needs or circumstances. The plan should then be updated and the agreed changes recorded and implemented.

■ The plan should be signed by the service user or a representative on their behalf and made available in a language and format that they can understand.

■ A copy of the plan is held by the service user unless there are clear and recorded reasons not to do so.

Standard 8 – Privacy and Dignity

■ Personal care and support of the service user should be provided in a way which maintains and respects their privacy, dignity and lifestyle at all times with particular regard to:
   – assisting with dressing and undressing
   – bathing
   – washing
   – shaving
   – oral hygiene
   – toilet and continence requirements
   – medication requirements and other health-related activities
   – manual handling
   – eating and meals

- handling personal possessions and documents
- entering the home, room, bathroom or toilet.

■ Care and support should be provided in the least intrusive way and service users and their relatives and representatives should be treated with courtesy at all times and addressed by the names they prefer.

■ Care and support workers must be sensitive and responsive to the race, culture, religion, age, disability, gender and sexuality of all people receiving care, and that of their relatives and representatives.

Standard 9 – Autonomy and Independence

■ Managers and care and support workers should enable service users to make decisions in relation to their own life, providing information, assistance and support where needed. Service users should be encouraged, enabled and empowered to control their own personal finances unless prevented from doing so by severe mental incapacity or disability.

■ Care and support workers should carry out tasks with service users, and not for them, minimising the intervention and supporting them to take risks, as set out in their care plan, while not endangering health and safety.

■ Communication with service users should always be in their first language or, where agreed, their preferred language.

■ Service users, and with their permission, their relatives or representatives, should be allowed to see personal files kept by the provider agency, in accordance with the Data Protection Act 1998. Service users should also be informed in writing that these files may be reviewed as part of the inspection and regulation process.

- Limitations on a service user's chosen lifestyle or human rights, if to prevent self-harm or self-neglect or abuse or harm to others, must be made only in the best interests of the service user. Such limitations must be consistent with the agency's responsibilities in law and any limitations imposed should be recorded in full within the risk assessment, and the plan for managing the risks entered into the care plan.

- Service users and their relatives or other representatives should be informed about independent advocates (or advocacy schemes) who can act on behalf of the service user.

Standard 10 – Medication and Health-Related Activities

- The care provider must ensure there is a clear, written policy and procedure which is adhered to by workers, identifying the parameters and circumstances for assisting service users with medication and health-related tasks, which should identify those tasks which may not be undertaken without specialist training. The policy should also include procedures if required for obtaining prescriptions and dispensed medicines and for recording the information.

- Workers should provide assistance with taking medication, administer medication or undertake other health-related tasks only when it is within their competence and they have received any necessary specialist training.

- Any assistance, administration or health-related tasks undertaken must only be with the service user's informed consent or that of their relatives or representative.

- Assistance with medication and other health-related activities must be identified in the care plan, and form part of the risk assessment then detailed within the plan.

- Care and support workers should leave medication at all times in a safe place which is known and accessible to service users or, if not appropriate for them to have access to it, where it is accessible only to relatives and other personal carers, health personnel and domiciliary care workers.

- Care and support workers must follow the agency's procedures in respect of medication administration.

- Any advice given to service users to see or call in their GP or other healthcare professional should be recorded and that record signed and dated by the service user (or someone on their behalf) and the care worker (*except for employment agencies solely introducing workers*).

- Where delivery of the care package involves multiple agencies, including healthcare, a policy on medication and health-related tasks is agreed and followed. A key worker, generally a healthcare professional from one agency who visits on a regular basis, is identified as responsible for taking the lead on medication, but care and support workers retain responsibility for their own actions in accordance with the policy. The agreed policy and procedures must be approved by a suitably experienced pharmacist, if appropriate, and the functions undertaken by workers in this context need to be covered by the employer's insurance policy.

PROTECTION (STANDARDS 11–16)

Standard 11 – Protection Safe Working Practices (except for employment agencies solely introducing workers)

- The agency must have systems and procedures in place to comply with the requirements of the health and safety legislation and the agency must have a comprehensive health and safety policy and written procedures for health and safety management.

- One or more competent persons must be appointed to assist the agency in complying with their health and safety duties and responsibilities.

- All organisational records relating to health and safety matters must be accurate and kept up to date.

Standard 12 –Risk Assessment (except for employment agencies solely introducing workers)

- Assessments must be undertaken, by trained and qualified personnel, of the potential risks to service users and workers associated with delivering the package of care (including, where appropriate, the risks associated with assisting with medication and other health-related activities) before the care or support worker commences their duties. Such assessments must be updated annually or more frequently if necessary.

- The risk assessment should include an assessment of the risks for the service user in maintaining their independence and daily living within the home. The manner in which the risk assessment is undertaken should be appropriate to their needs and views and those of their relatives must be taken into account.

■ A separate moving and handling risk assessment must be undertaken by a worker trained for the purpose.

■ A comprehensive plan should be devised to manage any risks identified within any area of care delivery and kept in the service user's home to which workers can refer.

■ A copy should also be placed on the personal file kept by the agency.

■ The risk management plan should be implemented and reviewed annually or more frequently if necessary, and a procedure should be in place for reporting new risks which arise including those relating to defective appliances, equipment or fixtures and security of premises.

■ In the event of care being required in an emergency, only workers who are both trained to undertake risk assessments and competent to provide the care are assigned to such a situation and *only* where pressure of time does not allow a risk assessment to be undertaken prior to the provision of the care.

■ If it has been identified that a service user requires two people for moving and handling, then two workers fully trained in current safe handling techniques and the equipment must always be involved in the provision of care.

■ The name and contact number of the organisation responsible for providing and maintaining any equipment under the Manual Handling Regulations and Lifting Operations and

Lifting Equipment Regulations must be recorded on the service user's risk assessment. The care organisation must ensure that the manual handling equipment is in a safe condition to use, that inspection by the manufacturers has taken place on time and, if necessary, remind the organisation providing the equipment that a maintenance check is due.

■ Safety policies and procedures must be in place to protect workers travelling to and from service users' homes including:
  – advice on not carrying large sums of money or medicines late at night
  – working in pairs
  – the use of bleeps/pagers
  – the use of mobile telephones
  – car insurance for business use.

■ A responsible and competent person must be on call and contactable at all times when care and support staff are on duty.

Standard 13 – Financial Protection (except for employment agencies solely introducing workers)

■ There must be policy and procedures in place for workers on:
  – the safe handling of a service user's money and property
  – payment of bills
  – shopping
  – collection of pensions
  – safeguarding property while undertaking the care tasks
  – reporting the loss of or damage to property while providing care.

■ The provider agency must also have guidance for care staff on *not*:

- accepting gifts or cash (beyond a very minimal value)
- using any loyalty cards belonging to service users
- making personal use of a service user's property, e.g. telephone
- involving service users in gambling syndicates (e.g. National Lottery, football pools).

■ Policy should also cover:
- the borrowing or lending of money
- selling or disposing of goods belonging to service users or their family
- selling goods or services to the consumer
- incurring a liability on a service user's behalf
- taking responsibility for looking after any valuables for service users
- taking any unauthorised person (including children) or pets into the service user's home without permission from the service user or their relatives, representative *and* the manager of the service.

■ The agency's policies and practices regarding any wills and bequests made by the service user must preclude the involvement of any staff or members of their family in the making of or benefiting from such wills or soliciting any other form of bequest or legacy or acting as witness or executor or being involved in any way with any other legal document.

■ There must be policy and procedure for the investigation of allegations of financial irregularities and the involvement of police, Social Services and professional bodies.

■ The amount and purpose of all financial transactions under-taken on behalf of the service user, including shopping and the collection of pensions, should be recorded appropriately on the visit record held in the home and signed and dated by the care and support worker and by the service user or their representative.

■ If a service user is unable to take responsibility for the management of finances, this should be recorded on the risk assessment and action taken to minimise the risk.

Standard 14 – Protection of the Person (except for employment agencies solely introducing workers)

■ Service users must be safeguarded from any form of abuse or exploitation including:
  – physical
  – financial
  – psychological
  – sexual
  – neglect
  – discriminatory
  – self-harm
  – inhuman or degrading treatment through deliberate intent
  – negligence or ignorance with regard to written policies and procedures.

■ The agency must have robust procedures for responding to suspicions or evidence of abuse or neglect to ensure safety and protection.

■ All allegations and incidents of abuse must be followed up promptly and the details and action taken recorded in a special record/file kept for the purpose and kept on the service user's personal file.

■ Training on prevention of abuse should be given to all staff within six months of employment and updated every two years.

Standard 15 – Security of the Home (except for employment agencies solely introducing workers)

■ Care and support workers must ensure the security and safety of the service user and their home and do so at all times when providing personal care.

■ Clear protocols should be in place in relation to entering the home which cover:
  - knocking/ringing bell
  - speaking aloud before entry
  - written and signed agreements on key-holding
  - safe handling and storage of keys outside the home
  - confidentiality of entry codes
  - alternative arrangements for entering the home
  - action to take in case of loss or theft of keys
  - action to take when unable to gain entry
  - securing doors and windows
  - discovery of an accident involving the service user
  - other emergency situations.

■ Identity cards must be provided to all care and support workers entering the home of service users and the cards should display:
  - a photograph of the worker
  - their name

- the employing organisation in large print
- the contact number of the agency
- the date of issue
- an expiry date which should not exceed 36 months from the date of issue.

■ The cards should be available in large print, should be laminated or otherwise tamper-proof, renewed and replaced within at least 36 months from the date of issue and returned to the organisation when employment ceases.

■ If a service user has special communication requirements, there should be clear and agreed alternative ways of identifying care and support staff from the agency.

Standard 16 – Records Kept in the Home (except for employment agencies solely introducing workers)

■ With the service user's consent, care or support workers should log on records kept in the home the time and date of every visit or the service provided and any significant occurrence. Where employed by the agency, live-in care and support workers should complete the record on a daily basis.

■ Service users and their relatives or representatives should be informed about what is written on the record and have access to it. Written records should be legible, factual, signed and dated and kept in a safe place within home, as agreed by the service user.

■ Records should be kept in the home for one month, or until the service is concluded, after which time they are transferred, with the service user's permission, to the provider agency or other suitable body (e.g. local authority or health trust, or other purchaser of the service) for safe keeping.

■ If a service user refuses to have records kept in their home, then they will be required to sign and date a statement confirming the refusal and this will be kept on their personal file in the agency.

MANAGERS AND STAFF (STANDARDS 17–21)

Standard 17 – Recruitment and Selection

■ Agencies should have a rigorous recruitment and selection procedure which meets the requirements of legislation, equal opportunities and anti-discriminatory practice and ensures the protection of both service users and their relatives.

■ Face-to-face interviews must be undertaken, on premises which are secure and private, for all workers (including volunteers) who are shortlisted and may be engaged.

■ Two written references should be obtained before making an appointment, one of which should normally be from the immediate past employer, and this should then be followed up by a telephone call prior to confirmation of employment.

■ Any gaps in the employment record must be explored.

■ New workers and volunteers should be confirmed in post only following completion of satisfactory checks which should include: verification of identity, work permit (if appropriate), driving licence (if appropriate), certificates of training and qualifications claimed, declaration of physical and mental fitness, confirmation service check by UKCC (if holding a nursing, midwifery or health visitor qualification), sex offenders register, General Social Care Council register.

■ New workers, including temporary workers and volunteers, should be provided with a written contract specifying the terms and conditions under which they are engaged, including the need to comply with conditions in the agency's Staff Handbook.

■ Workers are required to provide a statement that they have no criminal convictions or to provide a statement of any criminal convictions that they do have.

Standard 18 – Requirements of the Job (except for employment agencies solely introducing workers)

■ All managers and workers should be provided with a written job description and person and work specification, identifying their responsibilities and accountabilities along with copies of the organisation's Staff Handbook and grievance and disciplinary procedures.

■ The person specification should include the personal qualities required to undertake the work and the appropriate attitudes to be adopted. Activities which should not be undertaken by care and support workers should also be identified.

■ Workers are required to notify their employer of any new criminal offence they may have committed, including motoring offences.

■ Workers believed to have committed any offence prescribed by regulations should immediately be reported to the

Protection of Vulnerable Adults (POVA) or Protection of Children Act (POCA) list.

Standard 19 – Development and Training (except for employment agencies solely introducing workers)

- The agency should have a staff development and training programme, reviewed and updated annually. The training should ensure that workers are able to fulfil the aims of the agency and meet the changing needs of users of the service, their relatives and representatives. There should also be a structured induction process, which is completed by new care and support workers.

- The induction process should include a minimum three days' orientation programme at the start of employment which covers a range of topics (a list of which can be found in the original standards) and should include shadowing an experienced care or support worker prior to taking responsibility themselves for the provision of personal care services and working alone in the homes of service users.

- Specialist advice, training and information should be provided for care or support workers working with specific user groups and/or medical conditions by someone who is professionally qualified to do so. (A list of areas of specialist training can also be found within the original standards.)

- Within the whole staff group of an agency there should be the range of skills and competence required to work with and meet the needs of individual users of its service, and managers or supervisors of care or support workers providing specialist care services should have the knowledge and understanding of the specialisms for which they are responsible.

■ Refresher and updating training should be identified at least annually and incorporated into the staff development and training programme.

Standard 20 – Qualifications (except for employment agencies solely introducing workers)

■ All those working within the organisation should be competent and trained to undertake the activities for which they are employed and responsible.

■ Newly appointed care or support workers delivering personal care who do not already hold a relevant care qualification are required to demonstrate their competence and register for the relevant NVQ in Care award (either NVQ in Care level 2 or level 3) within the first six months of employment and to complete the full award within three years.

■ Managers of organisations should obtain a nationally recognised management qualification equivalent to NVQ level 4 and they should undertake periodic management training to update their knowledge, skills and competence to manage the agency.

Standard 21 – Supervision (except for employment agencies solely introducing workers)

■ All care and support workers should receive regular supervision and have their standard of practice appraised annually, and should meet formally on a one-to-one basis with their line manager to discuss their work at least every three months.

■ With the consent of the service user at least one of these meetings should incorporate direct observation of a care worker who regularly provides their care.

■ All workers should have an annual appraisal of their overall standard of performance and identification of training and development needs, and managers and supervisors should receive training in supervision skills and undertaking performance appraisal.

ORGANISATION AND RUNNING OF THE BUSINESS (STANDARDS 22–27)

Standard 22 – Business Premises, Management and Planning

■ The business should operate from permanent premises and there must be a management structure in place, including clear lines of accountability, which enables the agency to deliver services effectively on a day-to-day basis, in accordance with the agency's business plan.

■ The service should be managed and provided from sound and permanent premises which are suitable and designated for the purpose, which provide a safe working environment for staff and which include the provision of private space for confidential meetings.

■ The premises should be located appropriately for the management and provision of domiciliary care to the people it serves and be equipped with the resources necessary for the efficient and effective management of the service.

■ The management structure should reflect the size of the agency and the volume and complexity of the care provided, and the organisation must demonstrate that there is adequate staff cover for the operation of the agency.

Standard 23 – Financial Procedures

■ The agency must demonstrate that sound accounting and other financial procedures are adopted to ensure the effective and efficient running of the business and its continued financial viability.

■ Systems should be in place so that accurate calculations can be made of the charges for the service.

■ Insurance cover should be sufficient to protect the agency's assets and liabilities, including the agency's legal liabilities to any and all employees and third parties, e.g. service users, to a limit of indemnity commensurate with the level and extent of the activities undertaken.

Standard 24 – Record-Keeping

■ The agency should maintain all records required for the protection of the users of the service and the efficient running of the business for the legal requisite lengths of time to include:
  – financial records detailing all transactions of the business
  – a personal file on each consumer*
  – personnel files on each member of staff
  – interviews of applicants for posts who are subsequently employed

- an accident report record*
- a record of incidents of abuse or suspected abuse (including use of restraint) and action taken
- a record of complaints and compliments and action taken
- records of disciplinary and grievance procedures
- records kept in the home of consumers.*

(**Except for employment agencies solely introducing workers.*)

■ All records should be secure, up to date and in good order and are constructed, maintained and used in accordance with the Data Protection Act 1998 and other statutory requirements.

■ Consistent and standard personal data must be kept on all those being cared for by the agency (*except for employment agencies solely introducing workers*).

■ Service users must have access to their records and information held by the agency and they should be given access when necessary.

Standard 25 – Policies and Procedures

■ The agency must implement a clear set of policies and procedures to support best practice and meet the requirements of legislation. Such policies and procedures should be dated and monitored as part of the quality assurance process and reviewed and amended annually or more frequently if necessary.

■ Workers should understand and have access to up-to-date copies of all policies, procedures and codes of practice, and service users should have access to relevant information on the policies and procedures and other documents in appropriate formats.

Standard 26 – Complaints and Compliments

▪ The agency should have a well publicised and accessible procedure to enable service users and their relatives or representatives to make a complaint or compliment and for complaints to be investigated. The procedure should include the stages and timescales for the process.

▪ Positive action should be taken to encourage, enable and empower service users to access the complaints and compliments procedure, including access to appropriate interpretation and methods of communication.

▪ All complaints should be acknowledged in an appropriate form and the investigation commenced within the period specified in the information given.

▪ Complainants should be kept informed at each and every stage of the investigatory process and given information on the appeals procedure and for referring a complaint to the regional office of the Commission for Social Care Inspection at any stage if they so wish.

▪ A record should be kept by the agency of all complaints and compliments, including details of the investigation and action taken. This record should also be kept on the personal file of the complainant service user and kept in the agency and on the home care or support worker's personnel record.

▪ There should be a system in place to analyse and identify any pattern of complaints.

Standard 27 – Quality Assurance

■ Agencies should have an effective system for Quality Assurance based on the outcomes for service users and there should be a process and a procedure for consulting with them about the care service on a regular basis, assuring quality and monitoring performance including:

– an annual visit to each user of the service to be undertaken by a supervisor or manager and combined, where appropriate, with a review of the care plan or the monitoring of the performance of the care or support worker*

– regular supervision meetings between the line manager and care and support workers*

– an annual survey of all users of the service, their relatives or representatives where appropriate to obtain their views and opinions of the service

– checks on records, timesheets, etc.

(*Except for employment agencies solely introducing workers.)

■ Care and support workers should know the standard of service they are required to provide and monitor and meet that standard on a continuous basis.

■ The outcome from the QA process should be published annually and supplied to the CSCI and made available to service users, their family or representatives, and all stake-holders in the agency.

■ The standards and the QA process should be reviewed and revised as necessary, but on at least an annual basis.

Index